FUNDAMENTALS OF HOSPITALITY

FUNDAMENTALS OF HOSPITALITY

Neelendra Srivastava

NAMAN PUBLISHER & DISTRIBUTORS
NEW DELHI

Published by
Sangeeta Jain for Naman Publisher & Distributors
7360-B, Prem Nagar,
Gali No.1, Shakti Nagar,
Delhi-110007
PH: 23823642, MOB.: 09013478302
E-mail: rajivjain72@ymail.com

First Published – 2011

ISBN–978-81–920935–0-5

Published in an association with **HLDC**, Agra.

SOLE DISTRIBUTOR
JINDAL BOOK SERVICES
LG-4A, Ganpati Bhawan,
4675-B/21, Ansari Road,
Darya Ganj, Delhi - 110002

Jacket Designed by :
S.M. Graphics

Printed by:
Sachin Printers, Delhi, India

Preface

This book offers a historical perspective of the hospitality industry and covers all hotel operating areas to provide an understanding of each department and how it operates. The hospitality industry pays those well who have prepared well. Hospitality management involves the planning, organizing, directing and controlling of human and material resources within the lodging, restaurant, travel and tourism, institutional management, recreational management and meeting and convention planning industries. All of these separate yet related segments of the food service industry are interrelated to deliver kind and generous services to guests. The food service industry in the United States is booming and appears to be immune from the weak economy of the twenty-first century's first decade. Sales have increased from about $43 billion in 1970 to $426 billion in 2003. The National Restaurant Association estimates that more than 54 billion meals were eaten in restaurants and school and work cafeterias in 2002. In 2002 the food service industry employed about 11.7 million workers, making it the largest U.S. employer besides the government. Food and beverage service employment is expected to reach 13.3 million by 2012. The book consists of detail description about the varied aspects of basis of lodging and food service industry. The book is of tremendous significance for the people related to the field, researchers, students and teachers as well.

This book is designed and presented in an easy to read and easy to understand format. It will be beneficial to both aspiring professionals and those already in the industry.

We hope this text book meets its intended purpose as a practical resource, and serve as a vehicle for promoting the professionalism of this important segment of the Hospitality Industry.

NEELENDRA SRIVASTAVA

HERITAGE

LEARNING & DEVELOPMENT CENTER

Heritage Learning and Development Centre (HLDC) is an extended arm of Heritage Institute of Hotel & Tourism (HIHT). Heritage Institute of Hotel & Tourism is an Institute of excellence of the upcoming chain of Management Institutes, founded by D. K. Singh, President. At HIHT, our endeavour is to take education to the higher domains of never ending success. Heritage Institute of Hotel & Tourism provides the best possible infrastructure for pursuing best quality Hotel Management Education. HIHT has three campuses Agra, Shimla and Goa and proposed campuses at Kolkata, Pune, and Singapore.

In the modern era, Hospitality Industry is a reality, fighting for extremely challenging phase and getting into a stability mode. There are SMILES everywhere and this is relatively controlled and guarded, a sign of maturing and learning of Hospitality, which is cyclic in nature. The Hospitality Industry reflects a bright future. Earlier days, hospitality was synonymous with only hotel industry, but today this industry holds its important place with tourism. Hospitality academic in India is still in its nascent stage when compared to the west.

HLDC has been developed through the inputs from the industry and experts from the academics. This panel of experts have gone through the book and made suggestions which were incorporated. Every attempt has been made to thoroughly cover the day to day problems faced in the profession. In this field, as in most any other, it is prudent to remember the old adage, actions speak louder than words. The information given in this book makes the students fit for the industry. It provides about technical skills, personality and soft skills and ability to think and make decision.

This book is designed and presented in an easy to read and easy to understand format. It will be beneficial to both aspiring professionals and those already in the industry.

We hope this text book meets its intended purpose as a practical resource, and serve as a vehicle for promoting the professionalism of this important segment of the Hospitality Industry.

Contents

1

Hospitality Services

In relation to hospitality provision the culture of service refers to the values and meanings which underlie hospitality and give it its essential quality. Essential to hospitality are the reception and entertainment of guests who are to be provided with psychological and physiological comfort and security. Hospitality includes both tangible and intangible services. When a service encounter takes place between a tourist and a waiter, both are engaging in the culture of service.

In performing the required technical skill for serving the food and drink, the waiter provides the tangible service. The social interaction between the waiter and the tourist is the intangible service and contributes to the tourist's total experience. According to Powers, the social interaction requires genuine warmth and friendliness and necessitates empathy.

Service provision is a situational social process provided at an appropriate level and catering for individual needs. This kind of labour in which emotion plays a key role is referred to as emotional labour. It as exploitation of emotion. It as labour that 'calls for the coordination of mind and feeling' for the purpose of producing 'the proper state of mind in others'. The establishment of a contrived emotional relationship through emotional labour is 'difficult and demanding, under-recognised and relatively under-rewarded'. The relationship is also an unequal relationship between the recipient of the service who is dependent on the service job for employment.

The actors in the service encounter bring to the interaction their own ethnic/national identities. Using the language of the computer age we can discribe cultural identity. This kind of culture as 'the collective programming of the mind which distinguishes the members of one group or category of people from another'. The programming involves the establishment within the person of 'patterns of thinking, feeling, and potential acting' which Hofstede calls 'the software of the mind'. Culture of this kind is learned from the various groups within which a person interacts during the course of his or her lifetime. The family, for example, plays a major role in the cultural development of an individual. According to Hofstede, much of this cultural development is acquired during early childhood 'when a person is most susceptible to learning and assimilating'.

Cultural differences are demonstrated in a variety of ways. In some societies, for example, great respect is accorded to age to a degree not evident in other societies. Ideas about personal space vary from culture to culture. In some cultures, making eye contact during verbal communication is unacceptable; in other cultures eye contact is important as a sign of openness. These various examples of cultural difference are generalisations. Besides belonging to cultural groups people are also unique personalities. Uniqueness does not, however, diminish the importance of culture. Uniqueness does know bounds; these bounds are set by the cultural groups with which individuals identify.

While language differences are likely to be the most obvious component of cross- cultural service encounters, there are other aspects of Hofstede's 'software of the mind' that need to be taken into account. For example, what 'collective programming of the mind' has taken place to influence the attitude of a young man or woman towards the desirability of being a waiter in a restaurant? Anecdotal evidence from Southeast Asian tourism and hospitality students in Australia suggests that such a job is not considered desirable for its own sake.

Instead it is seen as a way to make money for immediate living expenses and, in the long term, as a springboard for a managerial position. In some cases there is reluctance to learn what are considered to be the more menial hospitality skills. If the job is not highly regarded within the cultural group, how will this affect the waiter's enthusiasm for and performance in the job? There is also the likelihood that the 'collective programming of the mind' has included animosity between cultural groups. Will this animosity affect the service encounters between members of those groups?

The major issues associated with the cultural dimensions of service. The service received in a host country is often judged by the tourist's own cultural standards. For example, the Asia Pacific region is host to approximately 10 million Japanese tourists each year. There is a great chance that visitors to the region will find customer contact people either unaware of or unable to respond to their clients' needs. Tourists in foreign lands are likely to be in search of cultural knowledge and experience. Whilst this knowledge and experience is formally provided by tour operators and guides they employ, informally hospitality service providers such as waiters and receptionists may, through conversations with guests, serve as another source of cultural knowledge.

Anecdotal evidence from tourists who have visited Bali, for example, indicates service encounters in restaurants during which young Balinese waiters, anxious to practise their English, engage with guests in the exchange of knowledge about their respective cultures. In some cases friendships are formed, correspondence is exchanged and contacts are renewed on repeat visits to Bali. In the anthropological literature, the waiter performing this role is described as a culture broker. 'Culture brokers are found in all cross-cultural situations... amongst taxi drivers, tourist guides, tourist police, security guards, hotel workers and market vendors. They act as mediators between tourists and the resident population'. In this capacity they play an important part in enhancing the tourists' experience of a destination.

Organisational Culture

The way that management mobilises combinations of values, language, rituals and myths' in order to unlock 'the commitment and enthusiasm of employees'. The outcome of a positive organisational culture in terms of the employees 'sense of belonging to the organisation' combined with 'a sense of enrichment in the job, and confidence in management'. Critical concept of organisational culture and its links with commitment, arguably it may be possible to draw from their descriptions dimensions of organisational culture appropriate to large and small enterprises which provide hospitality services.

If the idea is accepted that the service encounter has the potential to provide intangible as well as tangible benefits, it would seem to follow that management should have in place the appropriate 'combinations of values, language, rituals and myths' to encourage 'the commitment and enthusiasm of the employees' in enhancing the tourist's total experience.

When service is examined within the context of hospitality organisations, it can calls affective and continuance commitment responses from employees. Positive feelings of identification and involvement with their organisation develop an emotional attachment to it. This results in employees wanting to maintain their tenure, relate positively to their customers and provide the customer with quality service. Service as involving intimacy with the customer as well as a concern in providing a quality service for the consumer. Terms continuance commitment where employees, through longevity of service and past promotions, feel trapped in their employment. If these employees left their organisation it would be at great financial and personal cost to themselves and their plateaued careers.

Continuance commitment people were found to relate less positively, and in some cases, even negatively to their customers as well as doing no more than was necessary to maintain their membership of the organisation. Those organisations that succeed in winning emotional commitment from their employees and engage in career development are likely to be better service providers than those that have employees who feel trapped with nowhere to go. For people serving time in their organisation their own needs may become more important than serving the customer.

Human Resource Development (HRD)

Human Resource Development has improved performance as its ultimate goal in order to enhance the competitiveness and efficiency of an organisation. The term HRD is made up of three core components:

— training to improve the performance of employees in their current job,

— education to develop the whole person for future roles and responsibilities which as yet remain unknown,

— and development which prepares people for their responsibilities in the short to medium term of their career.

As tourism and hospitality is one of the largest and fastest growing industries in the world, it has, in the view of the WTTC, a need to address increased and improved tourism education in the region. This step is necessary in order to accommodate and adapt to ever increasing pressure on tourism and hospitality resources in the region. HRD is one of the most widely used terms in Asia-Pacific gatherings because it is seen as central to the competitive edge of the economy of a nation.

The key HRD stakeholders in any country are its HRD providers, supporters and users in terms of government, employers, and educational institutions. Tourists also are indirectly stakeholders in that they receive the benefit or otherwise of the outcomes and effectiveness of HRD initiatives. Governments will not become involved in HRD initiatives unless they believe tourism can make a positive contribution to their economy. As tourism employs 1 in 9 of the work force of the world, and it is predicted by 2005 to contribute some 2. 0 trillion dollars from travel and gross output in the Asia Pacific region, it would seem good economic sense for government to support well constructed arguments for quality improvements in the industry.

Technical skills are not the only component of hospitality service encounters, in any HRD strategy they obviously cannot be ignored. Ideally the development of a programme for skills development should be a joint project for industry and vocational education which together bring to the task an understanding of the requirements of industry and an appreciation of the pedagogical factors involved in providing training for skills development. The refinement of competency—based modules and train the trainer programmes in recent years means that standardised training can take place in vocational education institutions and in the workplace through on - the -job training.

Within the domain of skills development, there i5 the opportunity to empower employees by engaging them in a process of commitment to quality service When skills are applied within a Quality framework, these can be used to achieve satisfying service outcomes. If employees are engaged actively in continually improving their service processes to meet the needs of their customers, hospitality service provision will be the beneficiary. For example, through their direct contact with customers in a bar, hospitality staff may become aware that long queues form no matter how expertly they perform their skills.

Because of their first-hand knowledge of the situation, bar staff, if consulted, may recommend a change to the work process such as a series of minibars within the establishment to reduce time pressures on staff and satisfy their customers. In this instance both the customer and staff experience satisfying outcomes.

Hospitality Status

Service work in hospitality has low status as an occupation. At the same time the customer contact aspect of hospitality, it has been argued, plays an important role in the total tourist experience. It therefore seems imperative to take steps to raise the status of the occupation. One way in which an attempt can be made to achieve this goal is through educational provision for careers in hospitality. While considerable attention has been given to management training, more attention needs to be given to the integration of operational training into educational programmes at degree level.

There are, no doubt, several ways in which this can be achieved. For example, a degree may be constructed by building a one or two-year programme at university on to a two-year programme at vocational college. Alternatively, a three or four-year degree programme may be taken concurrently with a hospitality programme at a vocational college. The latter approach has the advantage of introducing students to the culture of academic reflection from the beginning of tertiary study.

In university circles it is likely that combining vocational and academic study within a degree programme will meet with some disapproval. The old status division between working with the hands and working with the mind has not disappeared. The combination of the two strands within a degree programme, however, has many advantages. It supports an integrated career path for hospitality workers thus helping to overcome the perception that hospitality work is a dead-end job.

It enables students who, through a relatively poor academic performance at school, did not gain entrance to university to prove their capabilities at vocational college and then to have a second chance at a university education. Lifelong learning cannot be constrained by artificial structures in education. In the vocational college component of the degree, assuming that hospitality practitioners are employed as teachers, it puts students in touch with the 'real world' of hospitality.

In Southeast Asia, there is an obvious need to stay abreast of the changing attitudes and interests of the tourism market. Equally important, however, is to keep informed about the attitudes and interests of the host countries, which change as the local people become more financially stable and increasingly aware ot the value of their indigenous culture and natural environment.

Tourism is the single largest revenue producer in the world today, having surpassed the oil industry to claim that distinction. Presently, tourism—related businesses generate an estimated US$2 trillion per year. It is estimated that 15 percent of all jobs throughout the world are directly or indirectly related to tourism. In an effort to get a share of this lucrative market, governments and private developers everywhere are intensifying their efforts to attract visitors.

The most successful will be those who recognise the all—important premise that large-scale resort developments as well as eco-tourism projects must consider the cultural and environmental qualities of the area. Today's international traveler can choose from a wide array of vacation destinations. He won't fly halfway around the world to stay in a hotel facility little different from one he can find at home.

Thus, a distinctive image is crucial to stimulating visitor interest. Many of the areas throughout the world (particularly urban areas) are becoming somewhat homogeneous—if one were to be suddenly dropped in the middle of a typical big city, they might wonder upon the first visual impression, is this Singapore, Sydney, or Seattle?. However, creating a successful destination resort does not require building a fantasyland with a multitude of gimmicks to keep the customers entertained.

True creativity calls for taking the existing natural and cultural attributes of the environment and, with human ingenuity, blending them in such a way that the end result is extraordinarily pleasing. A traveler expects a pleasant change from his customary lifestyle. Producing a destination resort that will give him this change is seldom easy and never accidental. It calls for comprehensive planning, particularly at a time when people are becoming more and more aware of and sensitive to the problems tourism engenders, along with the benefits it brings.

Destination resorts can and should be developed in such a way that they serve as a means for enhancing natural assets and preserving distinctive cultural characteristics. When existing site conditions offer spectacular views or white sand beaches, the problem becomes one of protection and preservation. Without realistic planning, the environment can be damaged to the point where visitors are repelled rather than attracted.

The first step in developing a well—integrated master plan is to evaluate the existing conditions on the proposed development site. Depending on the site, and the available information, this evaluation may require surveys of topography, flora, fauna, soils and geology, water resources, and investigation of cultural resources, socioeconomics, and history as well.

Through this process, unique assets and advantages of the destination are identified, and problem areas are exposed. In this way, valuable natural and cultural resources are not only preserved, but are also utilized and highlighted as amenities of the resort development which can provide the distinctive image which the developer is seeking to achieve. At the same time, features which have been subjected to damage can be de-emphasised, replaced or improved, thus contributing to the overall achievement of quality in the development process.

The master plan is based on a predetermined carrying capacity which reflects optimum ability of the land and natural environment to accommodate man-made development. This necessitates devising ways to accommodate visitors so that they do not destroy, by overcrowding or by overuse, the destination resort's natural amenities and its unique cultural attributes—the very things the visitor wants to experience.

It follow, then, that the tourism master plan must incorporate solutions to pressing environmental and cultural problem. It must function in harmony with nature and in balance with the community. The resort operator who succeeds in reinforcing harmony between society and environmental processes possesses a goose that never stops laying golden eggs.

SHARED SERVICES IN THE HOSPITALITY

The traditional hotel company, comprised of owned, managed, and franchised properties has historically located accounting and finance employees at the property level, as well as at the corporate office. Traditionally all financial information has been sent to the corporate office for consolidation, data analysis and reporting, although the primary processing has taken place at the property level. Often, the different systems being used at the individual hotels have resulted in inefficiencies at the corporate level with many manual processes being required, including data re-entry, in order to complete a consolidation and prepare the necessary executive information. The relatively antiquated and cumbersome information systems at the corporate headquarters have further hindered the ability of users to receive information in a timely and cost-efficient manner.

A number of the major hotel companies are either considering or are already moving towards implementation of a shared services system. Factors driving this decision include a desire for growth, the need to outperform the competition, and the desire to satisfy both the company's guests and individual hotel owners. All of these factors—coupled with a need to reduce overhead costs—makes shared services a viable solution.

The shared services model can help to lower processing costs, create a customer-driven "center of excellence," consolidate multiple processing locations into one location and incorporate a "fee for service" approach to transaction processing. This model is geared towards repetitive transactions that can be somewhat automated or handled through mass processing. Personnel can be consolidated and spend more time on "value-added" tasks under this model. Management will then be able to spend more time on making informed decisions, as meaningful data will be more readily available.

Centralisation

Centralisation, however, introduces several new business challenges which must be addressed prior to implementing a shared services system, with the selection of current technology to support a new structure being one of the most important. The many pieces in the technology puzzle include the architecture required to support the central functions, the application software needed to best handle data processing and reporting, and the communication requirements between the service center and remote locations.

Each site will need its own Local Area Network (LAN), which will then be connected to the Wide Area Network (WAN). The WAN will connect all remote sites to the central service center, and the central service center to the corporate headquarters if they are separated geographically, and allow users to access data for the entire enterprise as appropriate. To access the data, communication lines from each remote site to the service center database will need to be in place.

The application software is also very important in the infrastructure of the service center. It needs to be functionally rich and powerful enough to handle processing and reporting for multiple entities which may have very different requirements. For example, a resort hotel may need to track more detail than a small hotel with no restaurants, and institutional owners may need different reports than a developer/owner. The system must track an abundance of information, but also be capable of segregating the information so that management can access only the key results they need. Management must have extensive on-line data access and reporting tools to assist them in decision-making and business planning.

Within the technology challenge, system security becomes an issue. When accounting functions including payables and receivables are being processed by a service center which is handling numerous owner's accounts, data integrity becomes a primary concern. A system needs multiple levels of security to ensure that data is secured, that appropriate access is granted only to the people who should handle the data and that audit trails are available for researching any discrepancies.

Challenges in centralisation

Possibly the biggest challenge in centralising transaction processing is determining the costs and savings from creating a shared service structure. Costs can range from new hardware and software purchases to relocation costs of employees reassigned to work in the service center. The costs must be allocated to those who will benefit from and receive services from the new center. The costs for the shared services model are easier to identify than the savings. The initial investment in the service center includes:

— Application hardware and software;

— The WAN and LAN costs;

— Rent and building improvements;

— Employee relocation and severance expense;

— Initial training and change management;

— Implementing the new structure.

The on-going costs include the training and procedure development, communication costs, payroll and other overhead expenses. The benefits of a service center are more difficult to assess than the costs as many are intangible, including the potential for providing easier access to more meaningful data. A shared service center also may result in more informed decision-making and an infrastructure capable of supporting increased growth. Placing a dollar value on such benefits can be difficult.

Other benefits, however, can be more readily quantified, including:

— Reduced total head count;
— Processing time per transaction;
— Improved customer service response times;
— Improved average days to collect outstanding receivables.

Depending on the current environment and the number of repetitive tasks, the savings will vary. Companies that depend on manual processing or have outdated information systems can realise the greatest savings. Companies that have numerous locations that handle the same types of transactions can also realise big savings. Economically, the shared services model can work. Initial investments can be allocated on a pro-rata share basis to each participating location. Ongoing costs can also be allocated based either on a "fee-for-service" basis or a flat annual fee. Along with the savings, these allocations make the centralisation structure a cost reduction tool for many organisations.

Companies adopting a centralised process structure under a shared service model often implement change management efforts along with new information systems. Together, the two initiatives create an environment for reducing operating costs and improving efficiencies. In developing a strategy for a shared service center, a phased approach is preferable. The first phase calls for a Conference Room Pilot (CRP), which involves a minimal set-up of the new hardware and software at corporate headquarters, and one or two remote properties brought on line to test the entire design.

Corporate implementation is followed by the second phase, the enterprise-wide roll-out. The CRP phase is designed to identify unique requirements and assess the risks associated with the service center concept. Detailed requirements, confirmation and design will be completed during this phase. The technical architecture will be implemented, selected business scenarios tested and change management efforts developed during the CRP. As part of the change management efforts, all newly centralised processes will be redefined. Workflow will be streamlined and current job descriptions will be revamped while new job descriptions are being defined.

During the next phase, Service Center Implementation, change management and process improvement implementation efforts will be the main focus. Newly defined processing methods will be implemented. All remaining untested business scenarios will be tested. Data conversion and testing will take place. The center will then go online and processing will begin. The next phase, Remote Location Implementation, will consist of the same implementation efforts from the previous phase, but will focus on the individual hotels. During this phase, an implementation team approach will be utilised. Small, highly focused teams will go to each remote location to quickly implement the centralised structure and bring them up on the new system. Change management will also be very important as the move to a shared service center often results in significant changes in the way the accounting and finance function is conducted at the hotel. In particular, the role of the hotel controller will likely undergo major change.

All locations need to be involved in the process of developing and implementing a shared service center. This was the most valuable lesson learned during the analysis of centralisation versus decentralisation in information processing. Determining what functions to handle at the local level—in contrast to the service center—was one of the most difficult tasks. Without assistance from the individual locations, decisions would be made in a vacuum reflecting only the perspective of the corporate headquarters. To be successful, organisations need early buy-in from both management and staff personnel in all areas within the company. The more involved each project team member is, the smoother and more valuable the transition will be. Clearly, hotel companies need to review their operations as they seek to manage properties better, cheaper and more efficiently. The shared services model offers great potential, particularly for large hotel companies with operations scattered across distant locations.

Cost savings from more efficient transaction processing can be significant, freeing capital currently used in "back-office" operations for other purposes, including strategic growth. In addition, a shared service center also creates the foundation for improved information available for management decision-making and customer service. In this way, a shared service center can contribute in a direct and material way to a hotel company's competitive advantage.

Programme of scentralising integration

In hospitality, the responsibility for a company's growth is frequently relegated to the sales and marketing people who must find ways to fill the additional rooms. This is often the case even if the expansion adds questionable new inventory to a brand struggling for consistency -or in the face of the company's preoccupation with other priorities. The ability of the sales and marketing team to deliver business and the operations people to produce bottom-line results will often depend on a well-orchestrated programme of system integration that improves efficiency, increases productivity and supports higher guest-service standards, particularly in a multi-property environment.

In producing a "systems solution," the challenge is to make technology work in a truly integrated way.

Traditional technology offerings tend to be architected for a single function (i.e., point-of-sale, food & beverage, security and the like) and mostly for a single property. Often these systems operate on multiple hardware and software platforms. Typically, these systems have not provided the necessary level of integration, having been developed without using progressive "open system" client/server concepts.

Consolidating and sharing data across properties was never considered during design and implementation of these individual systems. In the aftermath of a new business combination or multi-property development, a system approach must be considered, but only at the appropriate functionality and at the right price. And when it comes to making these choices, both functionality and price depend on the company's strategic business plan and organisational design. Three primary technology options are available: development of a Superbase, a shared-service center or a hybrid integration of these two approaches.

"Superbase" approach

For those companies willing to forego some functionality to maintain a lower cost structure, a system approach may include designing a wide area network (WAN) to an already existing local area network (LAN) at the property level. This approach provides a one-way information download from the property unit to a central site that incorporates a centralised super-database (Superbase), which connects the individual properties via a WAN. Each property's LAN essentially becomes a node on the cross-property WAN. The Superbase contains mini-databases for hotel gaming, and property transactions.

Either an Enterprise Resource Planning (ERP) system or an optional data warehouse could integrate the data by combining it from each of the other databases, providing a means for three-dimensional data cubing and transaction analysis. Prior to making the trek across the WAN to the Superbase, the data is accumulated in staging areas (located on each LAN), then translated and standardised into a common data format.

The solution is simplified if all of the properties to be linked share a common technological infra-structure. This is rarely the case, however. Once the data is in the Superbase, it becomes part of a set of databases. Getting the data to the Superbase in a common format, however, can be quite a challenge. This can be achieved by using a "universal translator" attached to the staging area on each LAN. This translator converts the data from the individual systems into a format that is used by the Superbase and is designed to be flexible enough to easily incorporate the constant flux of changes that the individualised systems go through in their lifetime.

The Superbase concept allows each property to maintain its individual systems with minimal cost overhead. The wide area network (WAN) provides the holding area for multi-property data. The WAN file server can be located at one of the properties or at the corporate office. As a result, there are few organisational changes and investment outlays. In addition, the Superbase is designed to be expandable. If a new data stream is added to a property, it would not be a major technological undertaking requiting several months of development work to link to the Superbase.

A translation protocol to interpret and standardise the data -and space on the Superbase to store it—is all that would be required. The data residing on the Superbase can also be easily funneled into a data warehouse for three —dimensional financial and marketing analysis. One of the biggest disadvantages to the Superbase is illustrated by the casino example in Scenario One. For the cross-property comp information to be used, it must be viewed on the Superbase, which is limited by the one-way interface from the property LAN to the WAN. In addition, the Superbase requires clearly defined business rules agreed upon by all properties as a result of consolidating data using one standardised approach.

Scenario one

Setting: A corporation owns three gaming properties in the same metropolitan area. Each property has varying technological infrastructures handling its data, but corporate management allows guests to combine credit redemption points so that they may be used across the three properties.

Scenario: A customer gambles at Casino I then visits Casino 2 where he or she also plays. The customer has earned enough combined value from gambling at both casinos to earn a free meal at a buffet. Eager for a new environment, the customer ventures to Casino 3 to redeem the buffet.

Problem: Several different transactions have to be made to three distinct systems at the three properties: one transaction to debit the complementary value (or "comp") from Casino I; one transaction to debit the comp value from Casino 2; one transaction to credit the player's account at Casino 3 so he or she can receive the free buffet; and finally, a last transaction to debit the player's account at Casino 3 for the amount of the buffet. This can become an accounting and reporting nightmare for each property. Since financial reporting can be quite slow, it may be days before the guest's account shows the correct account balance. Until the correct information is shown, the guest may potentially redeem his points again at the other casinos while waiting for the accounting system to catch up.

One-way integration solution: The solution to this scenario lies in the Superbase design and one of its primary components the sub-database containing the redemption transaction data. This sub-database is the centralised repository for all point and comp information. Using the proposed cross-property solution, casino managers who plan to market across their properties will no longer be able to manage comps from the individual property's casino management system. To assure that the proper accounts balance and the correct reporting structure is maintained in a real-time manner, all comp transactions must be initiated from the Superbase.

Two-way integration— shared service center

The second system integration approach addresses the concerns of the especially complex organisations that need to manage and manipulate enterprise-wide data with functionality extending to both property and corporate sites. This approach offers a two-way solution that is most often developed through a shared-service center design. While the upfront investment associated with this second option may be costly, the long-term return for a shared-service center may outweigh the short-term outlays - if the organisation and its respective properties can reach the required economies of scale.

Business functions, especially those in the finance and accounting arena, are prime candidates for a shared-service concept given the repetitive nature of these processes. Hospitality companies comprising a mix of owned, managed, and franchised properties have historically had accounting and finance employees at the corporate office, as well as at the property level. All financial information has typically been sent to the corporate office for consolidation, data analysis and reporting although the primary process has taken place at the property level. The different systems and processes used at individual hotels have often resulted in inefficiencies at the corporate level with many manual processes being required, including data re-entry to complete a consolidation and prepare the necessary executive information.

Scenario Two presents an example of solutions in a shared-services approach. In a multi-property environment, the shared - services model can help to lower processing costs, create a customer -driven "center of excellence," consolidate multiple processing locations into one location and incorporate a "fee for service" approach to transaction processing.

Similar to the one-way and hybrid integration approach, each site will need its own LAN, which will then be connected to the WAN. The WAN will connect all remote sites to the central service center and allow users to access data for the entire enterprise as appropriate. To access the data, communication lines from each remote site to the service center database will need to be in place. The application software, however, is key to developing the two-way integration approach for the shared-service center. Both the properties, as well as the shared-service center, need to invest in software that is capable of replicating data content.

Pros and cons - shared services

The two-way, integrated shared—services model is geared towards repetitive transactions that can be somewhat automated or handled through mass processing. Companies that have numerous locations that handle the same types of transactions can also realise significant savings. The shared-service model, however, requires major upfront investment in new technologies, as well as commitment to planning and organisational change processes. Developed in-house, costs can range from new hardware and software purchases to relocation costs of employees leaving their location to work in the service center.

The initial investment in the service center includes application hardware and software expense, the WAN and LAN costs, rent and building improvements, employee relocation and severance expense, initial training and change management expenses, and the costs to implement the new structure. The on-going costs include the training and procedure development, communication costs, payroll and other overhead expenses.

Scenario two

Setting: A hotel management company manages 40 properties in different locations. Each property has varying technological infrastructures handling its data, but corporate management is seeking to combine property purchases to realise significant vendor discounts through volume purchasing.

Scenario: A large wine distributor delivers the corporate-approved house wine to one property in California, while another wine distributor delivers the same corporate-approved house wine to another property in Washington state.

Problem: Different volume purchases have to be made to distinct properties by different distributors, but the original price negotiated with the producer (winery) remains the same. This becomes an accounting and reporting issue for each property to insure that each purchase is billed at the corporate negotiated price. Again, since financial reporting can be very slow, it may be days before the bill is verified with the accounts payable and purchase order to show the correct account balance.

Two-way integration solution

The solution to this scenario lies in the design of the shared-service center, and the functionality of its finance and accounting system. The property purchasing system and the corporate or shared-service system need to be aligned with each other to update the data on a regular and accurate basis. Using a two-way interface solution, the properties and corporate can view the correct price and total volume of purchases throughout the system at any point in time.

Hybrid integration

A third option is a hybrid of the Superbase and shared-service center approaches. Using a clustering or complexing structure within a confined geographical boundary, an organisation can enjoy some of the benefits of the two-way integration approach for a select number of properties, but without some of the costs associated with developing a shared-service center.

Using a WAN, this method processes information or transactions at one site/property for multi-properties in the local geographic region. What distinguishes this approach from the one-way Superbase method is the assumption that the combining properties use the same technology and business rules at the property' level. This can sometimes be found in a particular region or city where properties of a similar brand are standardised in their informational reporting and technology specifications.

Pros and cons of the hybrid approach

This method benefits organisations that adopt a regional

management structure. By linking a few properties to a central site, the organisation receives some of the two-way integration advantages without spending the requisite costs to develop a shared-service center. In addition, overhead and communication costs can be kept low while reducing some headcount. As supporting documentation can be kept within reach, operators can also receive the added benefit of knowing that back-up files and information is easily accessible. The drawbacks to the hybrid approach depend on the level of technology existing in the clustering of properties. If each property has its own proprietary systems, the cost for a hybrid solution may be more than the one-way Superbase approach. In addition, the regional structure does little to contribute to the enterprise solution the organisation still has the issue of consolidating multi-property information in an integrated fashion.

Service Quality in the Hospitality Profession

Generally services are intangible or at least much less tangible than physical goods or products. This lack of possession means that services generally cannot be owned in the same way that manufactured goods can, they can only be experienced, created or participated in, with the result that customers may find it difficult to evaluate the services rendered.

Essentially, 'pure' services are more concerned with a performance rather than an object and unsurprisingly this has engendered the use of theatrical metaphors to characterise service work, an example being Disney's wellknown use of 'back-stage' and 'on-stage'. Experts suggest that often the lack of a tangible product makes it difficult for service organisations to differentiate themselves 'since customers do not always understand what information is being conveyed by different competitors.' In response to such problems they suggest that service companies may seek to 'tangiblise' the intangible via such things as standardising the exterior and interior of buildings to create an image which customers will immediately recognise, a strategy pursued with considerable success by companies such as McDonald's.

Hardware can be broadly conceptualised as the physical product (for example, the interior and exterior of a hotel, its rooms, meals, beverages and leisure services). The software consists of the more amorphous notions of service quality, service delivery and the emotional interaction between the producer and consumer. Thus, it could be suggested that both the hardware and the software comprise the overall product and in the normative view held by much of the services marketing and management literature must successfully coalesce to ensure organisational success.

Nonetheless, it is widely recognised that within the notion of intangibility, service organisations which offer a product that is, 'intangible dominant', increasingly seek to differentiate themselves on the basis of the software aspects such as seeking high quality and 'authentic' service interactions for the increasingly discerning customer. The key feature of inseparability is the high level of face-to-face or voice-to-voice interaction between buyer (that is, the customer) and seller resultant from the simultaneous production and consumption within the service process. This process has been variously described in hyperbolic terms as the so-called 'Moment of Truth'.

Indeed, this dramaturgical view of service suggests that the organisation, via its front line staff, has to 'get it right first time' in order to ensure a flawless performance which will result in the customer returning to any given service business. More measured and less prescriptive accounts of the service encounter are concerned to recognise a number of elements which pose a range of issues for organisations. This is particularly so on the issue of quality assurance where 'the consumer finds it difficult to isolate service quality from the quality of the service provider'.

Organisations, then, may face significant problems in attempting to manage and control interaction between their front line employees and customers. These problems are given a particular focus when we recognise the notion of heterogeneity. Heterogeneity refers to possible variations in service quality due to the labour intensity of most service production, such that 'the quality and essence of a service can vary from producer to producer, from customer to customer, and from day to day'. As a result of this possible variance in employee-customer interactions, service organisations may face difficulties in ensuring uniform quality of service between outlets, especially in branded services.

One of the ways in which organisations have sought to resolve this problem is to reduce the human element in service production by the use of mechanisms such as Automatic Teller Machines in banking for example. An alternative to this approach is to 'industrialise' services, by breaking down service operations into minute and discrete simple tasks to enable semi- and unskilled front line staff to follow a routinised, simple, standardised and often scripted approach to each service encounter, typified by fast food outlets such as McDonald's. This approach has engendered a wide literature which can broadly be seen as polarising between those who see this paradigm as one to be admired and copied or those who excoriate its dehumanising effects.

Increasingly, in addressing this problem of heterogeneity, a key strategy adopted by many service organisations is extensive employee training and development. This involves organisations recognising and acting upon the idea of front line staff being crucial to organisational success and, as a result, supporting things like 'soft' HRM, internal marketing, total quality management (TQM) and empowerment.

Challenge of Service Quality

Service quality is more complex to evaluate than in the case of goods. Services are more difficult to measure and standardise and consequently establishing an instrument attempting to measure quality has become a central challenge for the delivery of good service quality and service companies' success. The challenge of evaluating service quality has been motivated by recent research which increasingly demonstrates the significance of service quality as a central factor of business success. Service quality has consequently become a focus of any management and marketing strategy and high levels of service are seen as a means for organisations to achieve a competitive advantage and position themselves more effectively in the market place.

Customers are also becoming more aware and critical of the alternatives on offer and rising standards of services, prompted by competitive trends, have increased customer expectations. However, service quality may well be increasingly critical to competitive success, 'defining what exactly is "service quality" is somewhat problematic'. Generally service quality cannot be objectively measured as can technical quality for manufactured goods and it therefore remains an elusive and abstract construct.

The characteristics of intangibility, heterogeneity and inseparability presented earlier also constitute a challenge for managers because they do not allow for an easy process of quality evaluation. More importantly, a customer judgement of a service depends as much on the service process as on the outcome, therefore customers' quality evaluation can be seen as depending on the production of services as well as on their consumption.

The services marketing and management field has displayed different views of how this construct might be assessed.

For example, Akehurst and Harrington in a review of managerial perceptions of service quality in UK hotels note two schools of thought—American and Nordic—which have sought to address this issue. Though they differ in the detail of their approach, both schools of thought largely adopt a common approach in seeking to group a range of quality items into dimensions.

Some of the researchers offer an important distinction in their identification of process quality, which is judged by consumers during a service, from output quality, evaluated after a service has been performed. These authors also distinguished between the physical quality, relating to the physical supports of the service, corporate quality, which involves the company's image and profile, and finally interactive quality, which refers to the interactions between a consumer, the service organisation and other customers.

Another type of model proposed a division of service quality into four dimensions: technical quality, integrative quality (the ease with which different portions of the service delivery system work together), functional quality and outcome quality. Other work identified that service quality could be distinguished in two main dimensions, functional and technical quality. Arguably though, the seminal work on quality measurement in services is the SERVQUAL scale, emanated from the American school of thought and aimed to develop a quality scale that would be applicable across different services. The five dimensions were named and described as:

— *Tangibles*: The appearance of physical facilities, equipment, personnel and communication materials.

— *Reliability*: The ability to perform the promised service dependably and accurately.
— *Responsiveness*: The willingness to help consumers and provide prompt service.
— *Assurance*: The knowledge and courtesy of employees and their ability to convey trust and confidence.
— *Empathy*: The caring, individualised attention provided to the customers.

Each of the dimensions contained four to six statement sets. The intent of the statement set was to provide a score for components of the dimension that could also be averaged to provide an overall score of the dimension. Each statement had a corresponding perceived quality score calculated by subtracting the perception score from the expectation score. As a result of a important research effort that this scale demanded, and because of its innovativeness and the contentious issues it raised, the scale has suffered various criticism.

The goal was to produce a generic scale which would translate consumers' quality judgement in any service setting: The instrument has been designed to be applicable across a broad spectrum of services. As such, it provides a basic skeleton through its expectations/perceptions format encompassing statements for each of the five dimensions. The skeleton, when necessary, can be adapted or supplemented to fit the characteristics or specific research needs of a particular organisation.

However, further replications of the scale to different types of services have clearly demonstrated that its presupposed universal nature was refutable. This does not necessarily mean that the scale should be rejected completely but rather that consideration should be given to its suitability to specific services and its necessary adaptation to new service contexts.

Hospitality has been a fertile ground for research with numerous different applications of SERVQUAL. Some of the analysis shows that the first dimension explains most of the variance observed therefore giving poor credibility to the four other dimensions and the multidimensionality of the service quality construct. Another study on hotels provided different findings from the previous application, and the reproduction of the SERVQUAL dimensions were not confirmed either. Researchers followed step by step the SERVQUAL methodology and created a new scale, named LODGSERV, which displayed only three dimensions: tangibility, reliability and contact.

To add to the confusion compared the SERVQUAL and LODGSERV scales and concluded that 'both scales fail to replicate the proposed dimensions and to provide content validity in this specific application'. Furthermore, another application of SERVQUAL to hotel and motel services identified LODGSERV but this scale simply replicated SERVQUAL to the context studied. The SERVQUAL format commented on high expectations scores observed. Some items were also classified as dissatisfies and were defined as elements which would cause dissatisfaction by their absence but would not influence customers' satisfaction by their presence since customers assume that they would be present.

Lastly, and most recently, surveyed 155 three to five star hotels in Australia using a modified version of the SERVQUAL scale. Survey aimed to test the reliability of the SERVQUAL model by establishing the number of dimensions of service quality in the hospitality industry in an attempt to determine which dimension is the best predictor of overall service quality. The amended version of SERVQUAL added eight items which were considered to specifically pertain to the hospitality industry and deleted three items. This customised version of SERVQUAL was renamed HOLSERV.

Based on this findings there are three dimensions of service quality in hospitality, employees, tangibles and reliability and argue that '...the employees dimension emerged as the best predictor of overall service quality.'

Generalisation of SERVQUAL

It is believed that the problems encountered in the limited generalisation of SERVQUAL might be linked to the particularities of the services upon which it was developed. Indeed, the SERVQUAL scale was built from the study of four commercial services, namely repair and maintenance, retail banking, credit card and securities brokerage. These services involve situations in which consumers buy a service for rational and functional purposes. The service delivery usually encompasses a short service encounter principally monitored by an employee and the delivery takes place in a limited environment.

Indeed, most tourism and hospitality services may potentially involve complex processes, multiple encounters and a longer involvement with the service firm. For example, the consumption of a tourist attraction involves contacts with different staff, with a multitude of tangible aspects (the attraction itself, décor, ambience, comfort, objects looked upon, rides) and the evaluation of different services provided (the attraction, restaurant, cafe, shop). Similarly, consumers using a hotel will come across a multitude of tangible aspects (the hotel, décor, layout of the rooms, atmosphere) and a variety of services (room service, cleaning, catering services, reception, bar, leisure centre). Therefore the encounters are multiple and varied and all need to be integrated in the evaluation processes of service quality. More importantly, these different service features imply that the nature of the service delivery might follow different patterns.

For example, in certain hospitality services the encounter with staff might remain relatively limited and the tangibles aspects might be quite important suggesting that the evaluation processes could be based on different criteria. This recognition of diversity is believed to be at the centre of the SERVQUAL controversy. It is recognised that the potentiality to build a generic scale is unrealistic since it would wrongly suggest that services display similar service delivery features and that customers would use similar criteria to evaluate service quality. In fact, recognition of the limits of SERVQUAL to represent the diversity of services has already been recognised by several authors.

If other services categories had been included (in the SERVQUAL scale), particularly professional services which are high in terms of opportunities for consumer intervention and adaptation, it is possible that other factor groupings would have emerged, possibly associated with one or more of the 'incorporated' dimensions: competence, credibility, security or knowledge for example.

The SERVQUAL authors believed they had built their scale upon services whose 'categories were chosen to represent a broad cross-section of services that varied along key dimensions'. However, SERVQUAL was in fact built on very similar services. Consequently, the SERVQUAL authors' conclusion that the relative importance of the dimensions identified were consistent across service settings, was considered as unrealistic. More importantly, these authors compared the relative importance of the SERVQUAL dimensions across services displaying different degrees of interaction and customisation.

The relative importance of the five SERVQUAL dimensions in four new service contexts: teaching, restaurants, health care and bookstores. The results showed that the reliability dimension always remained the most important predictor of overall satisfaction for all the services investigated. However, services appeared to display different importance ratings for the dimensions according to their characteristics: in high interaction—high customisation services 'knowing the customer' was rated as the most important dimension whereas in low interaction-low customisation services, 'reliability' and 'tangibles' were the first two dimensions. The importance of service quality dimensions would differ according to the service characteristic

Implications

While most of the existing literature examining service quality has focused increasingly heavily on personnel contacts with customers, within certain areas of hospitality, for example hotel services, the tangible elements of the hospitality product are also extremely important. This, in part, is due to the fact that when using those services, consumers will tend to spend a longer period of time within the premises than for other services. For instance, the tangibles of a bank or a repair company can be assumed to be of lesser importance to consumers because these are not central to the service provision but also because the consumers will spend a relatively shorter period of time within those premises. In the case of hotel services, it can be argued that since consumers will spend a longer period of time, tangibles will become a central part of the product consumption.

Indeed, the notion of product consumption is key here because in a hotel, compared to a bank, as well as the longer temporal dimension customers are also consuming the tangible aspects of the room, restaurant, leisure centre and so on as an integral aspect of the core product. This is less likely to be true in a bank where the tangibles would ordinarily merely provide a meeting place between consumers and producers, they do not represent the product which is being bought and consumed by the customers. A study on the determinants of service quality in airline services indicated that physical dimensions such as food quality or seating comfort were very important factors in service quality evaluations, again this was a service where consumers spend a relatively longer period of time in the physical space.

More importantly, a recent study on hotel services clearly highlighted the specificity of that service context: 'Services differ in the proportions of tangibles they contain. It would be reasonable to suppose that the importance of tangible aspects is higher in customer experiences such as hotel services, which contain a high proportion of clearly differentiated tangible components'.

Whilst hotels can be both labour and capital intensive it is the former which has often generated the greatest interest and initiatives: The modern hotel industry has tended to promote its obsession with customer service delivery standards while ignoring the need for the hotel product to meet the expectations of the customer. Put another way 'soft' human and interactional processes are promoted as the principle means of ensuring customer satisfaction to the extent that attention to the 'hard' elements of the hospitality product is diminished.

Customer expectations have evolved and that evidence points to an increasing interest in the quality of the product rather than the service. Scepticism of the need for organisations to consider the softer aspects of the service encounter, much of the work that has emerged in relation to more prescriptive accounts of service quality have tended to point to the human dimension. Thus, although the tangibles are perceived as being important, the human dimension through the employee service is also particularly relevant. In sum, customer perceptions of quality will vary from service to service and will, at various times, encompass different aspects.

Indeed, in many respects notions of service quality may be as much about consistent delivery to the specified offer, whether high or low specification. As a corollary, this review of the dimensionality of service quality clearly reinforces the notion that the relative importance of quality dimensions will change between a fast food restaurant and Michelin starred restaurant or a basic budget hotel and a deluxe hotel. Equally this also points to the obvious point that differing HRM approaches are likely to be appropriate to differing service settings and it is this issue which is now considered by firstly reflecting upon the relationship generally between competitive strategy and HRM before moving on to the service sector specifically.

2

Travel and Tourism Industry

Travel and Tourism depends on a wide range of infrastructure services - airports, air navigation, roads, railheads and ports, as well as basic infrastructure services required by hotels, restaurants, shops, and recreation facilities (e.g. telecommunications and utilities). It is the combination of tourism and good infrastructure that underpins the economic, environmental and social benefits. It is important to balance any decision to develop an area for tourism against the need to preserve fragile or threatened environments and cultures. However, once a decision has been taken where an area is appropriate for new tourism development, or that an existing tourist site should be developed further, then good infrastructure will be essential to sustain the quality, economic viability and growth of Travel & Tourism. Good infrastructure will also be a key factor in the industry's ability to manage visitor flows in ways that do not affect the natural or built heritage, nor counteract against local interests.

Travel & Tourism takes many different forms - from a trip only a few hours away from home to long distance travel overseas. A common belief is that most Travel & Tourism involves large numbers of visitors from developed countries travelling by air to destinations in emerging countries. In fact, in most countries, the domestic tourism market is larger than the inbound market. Of course, the social and cultural impact of inbound visitors is often greater than that of domestic tourists.

Whether tourism is domestic or international, it involves visiting a destination away from the area in which one lives and using the services available in that destination. Therefore, tourists' requirements are for travel services to reach their destinations and once there, for services such as shelter, water, food, sanitation and entertainment. What makes tourism special is that, many of these different products and services are often supplied by different operators: usually small or medium sized businesses in local ownership. This makes tourism a highly fragmented and diverse industry and so co-ordinated, industry-wide action is difficult to achieve.

The influence of Travel & Tourism's demand also extends far beyond traditional tourism companies, into upstream suppliers like aircraft manufacturers or food producers and into the downstream service providers for travellers, like retail shops. Despite the difficulties caused by fragmentation and lengthy supply chains, there has been a steady growth in environmental good practice across the industry in recent years. There are examples of - airlines and airports reducing pollution and noise impacts; cruise liners practising marine conservation; hotels implementing energy consumption and waste disposal programmes; car rental companies investing in increasingly fuel efficient fleets and railways sound proofing to dampen noise. The result is that there are a number of excellent initiatives in place designed to improve the environmental management of Travel & Tourism businesses. Of course, more needs to be done.

World Trade Tourism Council (WTTC) with 105 members is the global business leaders' forum for the Travel & Tourism industry. The WTTC have set in place an extensive strategy to promote a culture of sustainable development and have put in place a three-tiered structure for its achievement. In 1996 the WTTC, the World Tourism Organisation and the Earth Council, joined together to launch an action plan entitled "Agenda 21 for the Travel & Tourism Industry: Towards Environmentally Sustainable Development" - a sectional sustainable development programme based on the results of the Rio Earth Summit in 1992.

Since the launch of the document, the three organisations have begun a series of regional seminars to increase awareness of the conclusions, and to adapt the programme for local implementation. The programme has held regional seminars in London and Jakarta in 1997 and Victoria Falls and Dominica in 1998. WTTC has recently introduced a major addition to the programme - the "Alliance for Sustainable Tourism", which invites public and private sector Travel & Tourism organisations to record their Agenda 21 based activities on a central web site and commit to co-operation with all other partners. In order to develop the programme from global principles to community based action, WTTC is also discussing with the International Council for Local Environment Initiatives (ICLEI) on how the principles of "Agenda 21 for Travel & Tourism" can be built into Local Agenda 21 programmes. Furthermore, WTTC is considering pilot projects in 5 cities around the world to serve as models for other destinations.

In 1994, WTTC initiated the "GREEN GLOBE", an Agenda 21 based industry improvement programme, which provides guidance material and a certification process linked to both ISO standards and Agenda 21 principles. There are now 500 "GREEN GLOBE " members in 100 countries dedicated to improving environmental practice. The first certification has commenced with hotels groups in Jamaica and Manchester (UK). "GREEN GLOBE" has also developed a specific Destination Programme, which provides a methodology for Travel & Tourism destinations to implement sustainable development. The ultimate aim is that "GREEN GLOBE" will become the primary global standard of environmental commitment by the global Travel & Tourism industry and will be recognised by the public as such. Currently, "GREEN GLOBE" has the support of over 20 international industry organisations representing thousands of businesses world-wide and the support of the World Tourism Organisation, the United Nations Environment Programme and the Earth Council.

WTTC have also developed "ECoNETT", a web-site containing advice and data on good practice and sources of help and advice. "ECoNETT" is increasingly recognised as a focal point for environmental information, good practice, new techniques and technologies. The International Hotel & Restaurant Association (IH&RA), based in Paris, represents over 700,000 establishments in more than 150 countries. Its membership comprises some 50 national and international hotel and restaurant chains, over 110 national hotel and restaurant associations, independent hotel operators and restaurateurs, industry suppliers and 130 hotel schools.

The IH&RA has offices in Asia-Pacific and Latin America. It is also the voice of the world's hotels and restaurants and plays a global role in representing, protecting, promoting and informing the industry to enable its members to achieve their business objectives. The IH&RA has:

— raised environmental awareness and developed programmes through joint workshops with national hotel associations and regularly encouráges them to develop their own environmental awareness programmes;

— established an annual Environmental Award sponsored by American Express and judged by the United Nations Environment Programme (UNEP) that recognises efforts by independent and chain hotels to "green" the industry;

— published advice including practical publications such as the "Environmental Action Pack for Hotels" with the International Hotel Environment Initiative and UNEP and "Environmental Good Practice in Hotels" with UNEP;

— supported regional initiatives such as the Caribbean Action for Sustainable Tourism; and

— joined forces with UNEP and the International Hotel School Directors' Association to develop an "Environmental Teaching Resource Package for Hospitality Educational Institutes".

The International Hotel Environment Initiative (IHEI), based in London, England, is a programme of The Prince of Wales Business Leaders Forum. Founded in 1992 by a consortium of chief executives from 10 multinational hotel groups, IHEI is an educational charity designed to encourage continuous improvement in the environmental performance of the global hotel industry. It does this through:

— raising environmental awareness in the hotel industry by promoting good practice internationally;

— developing hotel-specific guidance, enabling hotels of all sizes to implement environmental programmes; and

— multiplying the reach and impact of IHEI by working with partners, including hotel associations, governments, NGOs, tourism bodies and businesses.

IHEI is a catalyst and conduit for hotels to pool their resources and to share experience via a noncompetitive platform. In 5 years it has evolved into an organisation with global impact. IHEI has worked in 111 countries, stimulating and assisting with the establishment of local initiatives such as New Zealand's "Environmental Hotels of Auckland, the Asia Pacific Hotel Environment Initiative" and the Caribbean Action for Sustainable Tourism. Member hotels now represent over 1 million guest rooms and more than 8,000 hotels on 5 continents. The Co-operative Research Centre for Sustainable Tourism, based in Australia, was established in 1997 to enhance the strategic knowledge available to the Travel & Tourism industry through:

— long-term high-quality scientific and technological research which contributes to the development of an internationally competitive tourism industry;
— strengthening the links between research and its commercial and other applications;
— promoting co-operative research; and
— stimulating education and training, particularly in graduate programmes, through active involvement of researchers from outside the higher education system in educational activities, and of graduate students in major research programmes.

The number of initiatives undertaken by individual companies is large. The hotel has undertaken measures in the following areas to ensure that its operations are more sustainable:

— cultural and social - hotel employment, providing community infrastructure and development;
— natural environment - soil erosion measures and planting forests;
— pollution - sewage, solid waste and noise pollution reduction programmes; and
— environmental communication - construction of an Eco Park where all waste is treated within the park, a dry debris sorting centre, a lecture room to promote

environmental awareness and a sustainable development library.

Role of Agents and Partnerships

The public sectors, particularly national and local government, have an important role to play by setting the agenda and providing the framework in which action should take place. The regulatory environment also plays an important role in creating the conditions suitable for sustainable tourism. Self-regulation involving the agreement and co-operation of industry is always likely to be the most effective solution. Therefore, the role of trade associations and industry organisations in distributing information among their members and encouraging participation is essential. The major partnerships to be formed are between:

— *industry and the public sector*: to ensure consistency with the framework;

— *industry and the voluntary sector*: to tap into the enormous resources of expertise and good will that this sector is able to generate; and

— *industry and the public*: both travellers themselves and the people who live in the places they visit to develop more sustainable forms of tourism.

The industry is already doing much to improve its performance in terms of sustainable development. The challenge for the new millennium is to move from the existing ad hoc approach to a more systematic one. To do this will involve a partnership between industry and national governments to deliver the following:

(i) Governments:

— Integration of travel and tourism policy into broader government policies, especially the environment;

— Incentives for the Travel & Tourism industry, backed up where necessary by effective regulation.

(ii) Public/Private partnership:

— Infrastructure planned and developed with a long-term view and within a reference framework based on Agenda 21;

— Indicators and environmental impact assessment tools to enable effective local management and appropriate development.

(iii) International bodies:

— Co-ordination at an international level of environmental action undertaken by all sectors of the Travel & Tourism industry;

— Review of existing voluntary initiatives to improve the quality of reporting, their transparency and credibility, and the assessment of their contribution to sustainability.

(iv) Companies:

— Commitment to place sustainable development issues at the core of the management structure;

— Innovation of process and application through new technology;

— Commitment to education and environmental training of staff.

Consumer Behaviour

At the 1998 World Travel Market, WTTC hosted, as a part of its Environmental Awareness Day, a seminar entitled "Does the Consumer Care?" At this event, MORI presented the latest findings from their Business and the Environment survey - an annual UK survey devoted to public attitudes to the environment. The survey is now in its tenth year and illustrates the challenge facing the Travel

& Tourism industry in influencing consumer behaviour to promote sustainable tourism. Travel & Tourism is now more associated with environmental damage than it has been in the past.

The industry's economic success is not dependent on its green record - public sensitivity to environmental problems on holiday/business trips has not increased and is no more of a deterrent to repeat travel than it was previously. There is a downward trend in the public's willingness to pay extra for environmental protection and environmentally friendly products, including "green" Travel & Tourism. Awareness of companies making environmental commitments is only marginally up. Therefore, the challenge is to persuade the consumer that it is in their interests to adopt and promote a sustainable approach in their activities and purchasing decisions. Education programmes and the development and widespread acceptance of codes of conduct are useful tools in achieving this step. Once this message has been conveyed, it is then important to back this up with the necessary information to enable consumers to make informed choices. It is here that "ecolabels" and award programmes have value.

Environmental Education Programmes

The Foundation for Environmental Education in Europe (FEEE) seeks to promote environmental education by carrying out campaigns and improving awareness of the importance of environmental education. It is composed of a network of international organisations. The FEEE (headquarters in Denmark) runs three major campaigns in Europe for providing safe and clean beaches and marinas. The award itself is given annually to beaches and marinas that satisfy a number of essential criteria in three separate areas: water quality; beach management and safety; and environmental information and education.

"GREEN GLOBE"'s Dodo Campaign, is based on a cartoon character, who features in 65 Travel & Tourism videos. Dodo explains and promotes the actions that visitors can take to reduce the impacts of their travels. The videos are aimed at children and are designed to be fun, whilst conveying important messages about sustainable Travel & Tourism. The aim is to have these videos shown on inflight and in-room television channels to raise awareness and influence consumer behaviour.

Role of Codes of Conduct

Codes of conduct are also used to try and influence consumer behaviour. For example, "Guidelines for Responsible Environmental Tourism" are prepared and distributed by the American Society of Travel Agents to all customers who book holidays through their members' branches. The Guidelines aim to "encourage the growth of peaceful tourism and environmentally responsible travel" and include 10 recommendations to encourage tourists to act responsibly and show respect for their hosts and the environment of their destination(s). The Pacific Asia Tourism Association (PATA) is an industrial association, which promotes the Pacific Asia area's Travel & Tourism destinations, products and services. PATA also serves as a central resource of information and research, travel industry education and training, as well as quality product development with sensitivity for culture, heritage and environment.

In 1992, PATA introduced its "Code for Environmentally Responsible Tourism" to strengthen the principles of preservation in the region. Businesses, organisations and individuals wishing to affirm their support for the PATA Code are encouraged to participate in the PATA Green Leaf programme. The Africa Travel Association has produced "Responsible Traveller Guidelines"; the Japanese Association of Travel Agents has produced the "Declaration of Earth Friendly Travellers" and there are many more examples of industry codes aimed at educating and influencing their customers.

Labelling Schemes

There are numerous examples of industry sponsored labelling schemes, whose aim is to recognise good industry practice and influence consumer behaviour into purchasing the labelled products. For example, the "Green Key, Denmark" certificate operated by the Hotel, Restaurant and Leisure Industry Association (HORESTA) has 56 criteria that includes environmental information, water & energy consumption and waste management. Special features also include ecological food products, outdoor areas, non-smoking rooms, and adaptations for access by disabled persons.

Awards Programmes

There are a number of industries that runs and sponsors award programmes to highlight and promote examples of good practice. For example, British Airways has run the "Tourism for Tomorrow" awards since 1992 to encourage action to protect the environment. The awards are directed at tour operators, hotels, national parks and heritage sites, and other activities associated with tourism. By selecting projects showing best practice in their field as role models, others are encouraged to follow suit and consider the environment in the everyday running of their tourism business.

The awards are run annually, with a winner selected from each of five regions and an overall winner. In addition, two special awards are made for mass tourism destinations. The awards are run in association with the British Tourist Authority, the Association of British Travel Agents, the Pacific Asia Travel Association and the

American Society of Travel Agents. Entries to the awards have been increases every year. American Express also sponsors a variety of environmental awards for international tourism organisations.

Change of Agents and Partnerships

A broad based approach is called for which requires Travel & Tourism to work with:

- national governments to raise the profile of environmental and social issues within the education system;
- NGOs to raise awareness of tourism issues in their work and activities and provide feedback to the Travel & Tourism industry;
- development organisations to communicate with host communities to understand their needs and requirements;
- local authorities to engage local people through the inclusion of tourism issues in Local Agenda 21 plans;
- national and international trade associations, labour representative organisations and training providers to increase awareness and training of staff in environmental and social issues;
- Travel & Tourism publications (such as travel guides);
- Travel & Tourism journalists to raise the profile of reporting environmental and social impacts of tourism among consumers and tourism businesses; and
- the Internet as a source of information for potential travellers.

Travel and Tourism in India

The tourism sector has immense backward and forward linkages in terms of both income and employment and can contribute significantly to the economy. An imaginative and innovative approach keeping in view the socio-demographic changes taking place world-wide and an efficient information system would yield better results. At the same time, the need for sound perspective planning with local participation is imperative.

In India, however, the sector has failed to receive due importance on the country's development agenda. Employing only 2.4% of the Indian workforce, the vast potential of tourism as an instrument of employment generation and poverty alleviation has tended to remain largely unutilised. Of the 625 million world tourist arrivals in 1998, India received a meagre 2.36 million or 0.38% of the total world tourist arrivals and only 0.62% of world tourist receipts.

Compared to other countries in the region India's performance in the sector has been rather poor. Major causes cited for the low performance are lack of professionalism, unhygienic conditions, poor infrastructure, lack of easily accessible information, lack of safety, poor visitor experience, restrictive air transport policy, inadequate facilitation services, multiplicity of taxes and the low priority accorded to tourism. However, despite its tiny share of world tourist arrivals, tourism in India has emerged the second largest foreign exchange earner for the country even though the mainstay of the Tourism industry in India continues to be domestic tourism.

Domestic tourists, who stayed in accommodation establishments, increased from 109.2 million in number in 1993 to 159.9 million in 1997, registering an annual rate of growth of 10%. That growth rate declined to 9.35% in 1999 when an estimated 175.4 million domestic tourist visits were recorded. The foreign tourist arrivals to India grew from 1.82 million in 1992-93 to 2.33 million in 1996-97, registering an average annual growth rate of 6.37% during the Eighth Five Year Plan Period. In first two years of the

Ninth Plan, the growth rate declined to 1.49% and an estimated 2.40 million foreign tourist arrivals were recorded in 1998-99.

The international tourist arrivals at world's top tourism destinations in comparison with India are given at table 1.

Table 1. World top tourism destinations in comparison with India, International Tourists Arrivals

Rank			Countries	Arrivals (in million)	%change	% of Total
1990	1995	1998		1998	1998-97	1998
1	1	1	France	70	4.70%	11.20%
3	3	2	Spain	47.7	10.00%	7.60%
2	2	3	Unites States	47.1	-1.30%	7.50%
4	4	4	Italy	34.8	2.20%	5.60%
7	5	5	United Kingdom	25.5	-0.20%	4.10%
12	8	6	China	24	1.00%	3.80%
8	7	7	Mexico	19.3	-0.30%	3.10%
27	9	8	Poland	18.8	-3.60%	3.00%
10	11	9	Canada	18.7	7.90%	3.00%
6	10	10	Austria	17.3	3.80%	2.80%
9	13	11	Germany	16.5	4.20%	2.60%
16	12	12	Czech Republic	16.3	-3.00%	2.60%
17(1)	18	13	Russian Federation	15.8	3.00%	2.50%
5	6	14	Hungary	14.7	-15.00%	2.30%
14	17	15	Portugal	11.8	16.00%	1.90%
13	16	16	Greece	11.1	10.00%	1.80%
11	14	17	Switzerland	11	4.00%	1.80%
19	15	18	China (Hongkong)	9.6	-7.70%	1.50%
24	20	19	Turkey	9.2	1.80%	1.50%
21	21	20	Thailand	7.7	6.90%	1.20%
		40+	India	2.4	-0.50%	0.40%
			Sub Total	449.3		71.90%
			Other Countries	175.9		28.10%
			World Total	625.2	2.40%	100.00%

A very large proportion of the foreign tourists, i.e. around 91.7%, visited India for holidaying and sightseeing, followed by business travellers who constituted approximately 5.1% of the visitors.

Although international arrivals are a small proportion of world tourist arrivals, international tourists have the longest stay of 29 days in India. This is reflected in the proportion of revenues being higher than percentage of world tourist arrivals. The foreign exchange earnings during the Eighth Plan period surged from Rs. 6,060 crore in 1992-93 to Rs 10,231 crore in 1996-97, achieving an annual growth rate of 13.99%. The growth rate declined to 10.99% in the first two years of the Ninth Plan and earnings in 1998-99 were estimated at Rs. 12,604 crore.

The sector provided direct employment to about 14.79 million people during 1998-99. The Ninth Plan envisages the Government playing a role of facilitator for private sector participation in the development of tourism. The Plan seeks to diversify the tourism product by encouraging rural and village tourism, pilgrim and spiritual tourism, adventure and eco tourism, indigenous and natural health tourism, heritage tourism and youth and senior citizens' packages. The outlay for the Central Sector in the Ninth Plan is Rs. 793.75 crore, comprising a budgetary support of Rs. 485.75 crores and internal and extra budgetary resources of Rs. 308 crores. The main schemes of the Ministry of Tourism relate to infrastructure development, human resource development and publicity and marketing.

Ministry of Tourism has identified 21 circuits and 12 destinations for development. Financial assistance is provided to State/Union Territory (UT) Governments for developing tourist infrastructure at these places. In first three years of the Ninth Plan, 779 projects have been taken up. It has been observed that many States, particularly in the North-Eastern region, could not avail themselves of the financial assistance provided under the scheme because they could not find the required matching contribution for projects prioritised under the scheme. There is a need for modifying the pattern of funding under the scheme to enable all such States to benefit from it.

The scheme stipulates transfer of land ownership in respect of those projects in the name of the Central Government. The stipulation is acting as a deterrent in the operation of the scheme as the States face legal difficulties in transferring the land ownership. Ministry of Tourism needs to take urgent action to waive the condition. The Ministry has envisaged an equity scheme for attracting funds from financial institutions but the scheme has not made much headway because the State Governments have not been able to put up financially viable projects. There is a need to evaluate the scheme.

Village and Rural Tourism

Rural tourism needs to be given an impetus by earmarking funds for pilot projects on the basis of a model plan for each State for the purpose. These villages can be taken up for priority development particularly if the projects can be linked with the restoration of heritage properties in the area. This would provide a boost to local performing arts and help conserve the local culture apart from preventing rural-urban migration.

Local people in the rural areas should be encouraged to participate in tourism related projects, which may preferably be formulated by the tourist officials in consultation with locals and NGOs. These projects could be in the nature of providing glimpse of the village ambience and the tourists presented with local cuisine, art and culture by persons in local costumes engaging in the daily activities of cooking, weaving, dancing etc..

Moderate, but clean, accommodations for tourists should be constructed by villagers in traditional design and architecture. Bank finances should be made available at attractive terms and conditions for promotion of such projects. Although the North-East could be developed as a tourist haven by virtue of its topographic advantages, diverse cultures and its pristine areas unspoilt by pollution, tourism development has tended to elude it. The Plan expenditure incurred on the schemes operated in the N.E. States has been only about 30% of the amount sanctioned during first three years of the Ninth Plan. The concept of non-lapsable funds, introduced to ensure utilisation of the funds, is meaningless if it does not translate into concrete development. A revision in policy is required.

India Tourism Development Corporation Ltd. (ITDC)

The financial performance of ITDC improved during the Eighth Plan period and the net profit after tax increased from Rs. 10.05 crore in 1992-93 to Rs. 55.80 crore in 1996-97. In first two years of the Ninth Plan the profit after tax declined from Rs.43.30 crore in 1997-98 to Rs. 10.81 crore in 1998-99. ITDC would be required to intensify its efforts for economy in expenditure and grabbing more business through new initiatives in the face of competition by private sector. On the recommendations of Disinvestment Commission, the Government has taken a decision to disinvest in ITDC. Expeditious action is required in this direction.

Tourism Promotion Policy

— A National Policy on Tourism was formulated in 1982 focusing on the development of travel circuits and assigned the responsibility of promoting international tourism to the Central Government and domestic tourism to the State Governments.

— Tourism was given the status of an 'industry' in 1986 and became eligible for several incentives and facilities including tax incentives, subsidies, priorities in the sanctioning of loans by the State financial institutions and preferences in providing electricity and water connections.

— Tourism was made a priority sector for foreign direct investment in 1991 making it eligible for automatic approvals upto 51% of the equity.

— A National Strategy for Tourism Development was evolved in 1996, which advocated the strengthening of an institutional set-up in human resource development, setting up of an Advisory Board of Tourism Industry and Trade (which has since been set up), the integrated development of tourist destinations and the promotion of private sector in tourism development.

— Tourism was granted 'Export House' status in 1998 making hotels, travel agents, tour operators and tourist transport operators eligible for such recognition entitling them to various incentives.

— In order to take advantage of the liberalised economic regime and the developments taking place around the world, a new National Tourism Policy is under consideration of the Government.

Action Points in Tourism Development

— Liberalise India's skies to increase air seat capacity.

— Have a visa-less/visa-on-arrival facility for tourists from selected countries.

— Improve and modernize airport infrastructure and services.

— Allow free inter-State tourist vehicle movement.

— Rationalise and reduce taxes for end customer to make destination competitive.

— Close down Government of India Tourist Offices located overseas and make publicity increasingly through Inter-net and other electronic media.

— Make tourism a national strategic priority for employment generation.

— Incorporate sustainability perspective in tourism development plans/projects to prevent the kind of environmental degradation that have taken place at Himachal Pradesh, Goa and Jammu & Kashmir.

— Provide impetus to rural tourism by linking village development with restoration of heritage properties.

— Create public awareness about economic and social benefits of tourism.

Tourism and Environmental Issues

Tourism is not just a potential victim of climate change. It also contributes to its causes. Beyond seeking a zero emission form of travel for holidaymakers, a significant capping of emissions from air travel could be achieved through the introduction of an aviation fuel tax. Aviation fuel is currently exempt from tax, unlike other transport options which are less carbon intensive.

While the International Civil Aviation Organisation (ICAO) is strongly opposed to the introduction of a tax, WWF supports the introduction of an aviation tax. Revenues from such a tax should at least be partially invested in sustainable transport options. Another intermediate solution is presented by schemes such as Climate Care which offer tour operators or holidaymakers the opportunity to pay a voluntary levy on air travel into a fund that supports renewable energy projects and forest sequestration projects. The levy is calculated on a kilometre travelled basis and the investment aims to offset air travel CO_2 emissions by implementing reductions in other areas of energy usage.

Large tourist developments can put substantial pressure on local energy supplies, especially through air conditioning or heating. Energy requirements are often met by fossil fuel plant thus increasing the greenhouse gas emissions of the host country. In addition, the energy efficiency of buildings is often poor. Through improved standards at the development stage, or through retrofitting, it is possible to achieve considerable reductions in emissions.

Influence of Climate Change

The tourism industry heavy reliance on the local environment and climate to sell holidays means that it could face serious challenges as a result of climate change. Global and regional temperatures are rising. The hottest year of the millennium was 1998 and the 1990s were the warmest decade. Climate models suggest a future warming of 0.2-0.3°C per decade and sealevels are expected to rise at a rate of 4 to 10 centimetres per decade. An increase in extreme weather events such as floods and storms is also expected. While the impacts of climate change on tourism will vary, it is already clear that small island states such as the Maldives in the Indian Ocean, an increasingly popular tourist destination, will be particularly vulnerable to sea-level rise.

Climate change is also expected to increase the risk of illness in several parts of the world and this may lead to a falling-off of tourism. More frequent periods of extreme heat will cause discomfort in many eastern Mediterranean resorts, where the number of days above 40°C is expected to increase. A decline in cloud cover in Australia will increase exposure to the sun s harmful rays and malaria is likely to re-emerge in Spain, the most popular Mediterranean destination.

Winter tourism may also be affected, as the Alps and other European skiing destinations experience less snowfall and shorter skiing seasons. These impacts will be especially pronounced in lower-lying ski resorts, and in places where commercial ventures are already marginal. Tour operators and countries that rely on tourism for foreign revenue need to take into account the potential impacts of climate change, not only in planning new resorts or upgrading current facilities, but also in terms of the long-term future of their business.

WWF believes that action must be taken now by governments, individuals, and the tourism industry to reduce the threat of climate change. Governments worldwide should meet, and ideally go beyond, the commitments made through the Kyoto Protocol. The tourism industry itself must take action to reduce its contribution to global greenhouse gas emissions. For example, in destinations, changes to energy supply should be introduced, creating a shift from fossil fuel to renewable sources of energy such as wind, biomass and solar power. This needs to be coupled with changes to planning procedures and laws, so that more opportunities for renewable energy sources can be developed.

More stringent efficiency standards and a compulsory energy rating scheme could also be employed in buildings, such as hotels. Transport to, from, and around resorts and within destinations, is another key area where changes could be made. The tourism industry should incorporate public transport and cycling infrastructure in resort plans as well as alternative low impact vehicle technology. Offering customers the opportunity to make a contribution to renewable energy schemes as a way of offsetting air travel emissions would also be an important step. Finally, an international aviation fuel tax should be introduced, and local or short-haul holidays may be preferable in certain instances.

Environment and Air Travel

Travel by air is becoming almost as commonplace in the 21st century as walking was for our ancestors. Whether on business or for pleasure we fly, at the click of a mouse, to the four corners of the earth. Furthermore, thanks to travel search engines and low cost airlines, we even decide to go, not to a place of choice, but to where the cost is least. These are extraordinary freedoms. Air travel and airfreight are, at the same time, sinews of a growing, internet-linked, just-in-time, global economy. The growth is explosive. Since 1949, the birth year of the first passenger jet, air travel has grown seventy-fold. Britain has always been a world leader in aviation.

Today through its airlines, aerospace industries, its role in new thinking about air safety and security, and the great international hub of Heathrow, the country is a global player. But this position has not been won without cost to the environment. Britain's skies are noisy, its airports are hotspots of pollutants emitted by both planes and surface vehicles and as the number of flights increases, so do the acres dedicated to and blighted by aircraft operations. Yet compared with many of our Continental neighbours, where airports have been built or expanded to match demand, we have used operational efficiency to squeeze more and more use from existing runways. Since the end of the Second World War, the only completely new runway to have been built is Manchester's number two.

The London airport system is, as a result, one of the most constrained in the world. Constraint means congestion and with it delays, unreliable services, reduced efficiency, increased pollution and waste. Airlines lose revenue and costs rise for travellers, airports and all involved in flying. Such a situation is dangerous. Unless congestion is met by investment in new airport capacity there is a risk that Britain's air transport industry will become less competitive leading to damage to the economy. The forthcoming aviation White Paper will provide Government with an opportunity, for the first time in twenty years, to set out a new direction for air transport policy and to make long-term provision for airport capacity.

Aviation contributes to the British economy via air transport industries that employ over 500,000 and through firms, ranging from exporters of medical technology to travelling businessmen, which make use of their services. Aviation's growth has been the result, in turn, of the expansion of national and global economies which has led first to the movement of more goods and people, and, second to a fall, in real terms, of freight tariffs and travel costs.

The emergence in Britain of Europe's largest set of air charter firms is just one reflection of this growth. Wider benefits include stronger international trade links, wider transfer of research findings and speedier responses to natural disasters. A more detailed examination of how aviation affects the national economy reveals that airlines, airports and their supporting services make direct contributions; indirect contributions are made by off-airport activities such as hotels and tour operators; while decisions, for instance, to place investment in Britain because of its air links, count as contributions that are induced.

It is particularly noteworthy that "knowledge-based" jobs - a highly significant component in the new economy - tend to be those that can locate anywhere and are thus highly responsive to the availability of a good air transport hub. It should, furthermore, be noted that growth in air transport in the UK has taken place in a more open market than on the Continent.

— *Aviation jobs*: Reference has already been made to the 500,000 jobs that depend directly or indirectly on aviation. Expansion in air transport can be expected to cause this total to increase or, at least, to remain stable. But should Britain lose ground to France, Holland or Germany then a decline in such jobs must be a possibility.

— *Aviation Passengers*: The Government forecasts that demand for air travel in southeast England will rise from 117 million passengers in 2000 to about 200 million in 2015 and 300 million in 2030. Despite larger aircraft and developments in air and ground traffic control, it is not expected that this growth could be handled on existing runways. Additional capacity at Heathrow, Gatwick and Stansted, or even a new airport in the Thames Estuary, are therefore under consideration. Britain, as a gateway to Europe for the Americas, India and elsewhere, handles multitudes of transit passengers who in turn help raise the occupancy (and profitability) of connecting European and domestic flights.

  Nearly 200 million passengers transited in 2002 and over a third passed through Heathrow. London's hub airport, and the operating base of British Airways, accordingly handles more international passengers than any other airport in the world. Paris, Amsterdam and Frankfurt, all of which have recently seen heavy investment, eye this business jealously.

— *Aviation and Commerce*: About a third of Britain's exports, worth some £60 billion, are air freighted every year while businessmen and women make about 6 million flights. Both activities contribute to the country's gross domestic product. Reliance on air transport has, furthermore, increased steadily over the years and there is little reason to expect this trend to turn. It follows that Britain's interests are best served by a prosperous aviation sector that seeks to meet demand for its services. To what extent the White Paper will enable this growth to be met and how its environmental impacts will be abated, will therefore be central to the long-term health of the British economy

Technical Solutions

Everyone accepts that aviation's environmental damage must be minimised and its further growth made 'sustainable'. Emissions trading within and between industries is, meanwhile, increasingly seen as the best way to internalise the external costs of air transport all other activities. Trading promises to reduce pollution overall by eliminating first those sources that can be most inexpensively terminated while leaving those responsible for hard-to-treat emitters, such as aircraft, with time to develop the means to do so.

Environmental issues are, however, becoming ever more pressing. Not only is aircraft noise at airports generating increased opposition but pressure on governments and industry to cut greenhouse gasses mounts apace. Today's jet engines may be less noisy and more fuel efficient than their predecessors but, because there are so many more of them, fuel consumption and the noise affecting people living near airports are greater. It is thus far from true to say that technical progress has cut the overall environmental impact of aviation.

Reducing noise: The most contentious aspect of airport expansion is noise. Airports both attract and repel. Over time people are attracted by the prospect of jobs to live nearby. Meanwhile flight numbers grow and airport owners, in order to maximise the use of their costly assets, push as far as they can for 24 hour operation. None of this makes them good neighbours as demonstrated by recent legal actions against night noise in London.

Engines themselves are one source of aircraft noise but, as an airliner comes in to land, so is the roar of turbulent air over flaps and, above all, landing gear. The International Air Transport Association can claim that the average aircraft is now 20 decibels quieter than 30 years ago but if, on landing, the interval between successive flights shrinks, the exposure to noise of those underneath remains at best constant and at worst it is increased.

Containing noise is a major challenge for air transport. Three kinds of action are possible.

— Land use planning may be used to put distance between people and flight paths.

— Air traffic control can be used to route aircraft via the least populated flight paths - though this can increase fuel consumption and carbon emissions.

— Noise can be reduced at source by changes in engine design and aircraft aerodynamics.

Noise prospects: Future aircraft are forecast to be substantially quieter than the quietest models of today. NASA's 'Quiet Aircraft Technology' programmeme, for instance, aims to reduce the perceived noise of future subsonic aircraft by 50 per cent in ten years and 75 per cent in 25. But noise could be cut more quickly by reducing the age of the aircraft fleet. Given that the 'noise footprint' of today's new jets is less than 15 per cent of the oldest in use, updating the fleet would be highly effective. However this would cost money and is not happening. Although the world aircraft fleet has tripled in size over the past 25 years its average age has remained at about 11 years.

Reducing fuel consumption and emissions. Modern jets burn kerosene and together consume 3 to 4 per cent of fossil fuel production. When burnt in a jet engine kerosene produces carbon particles, water vapour and nitrogen oxides. These pollutants help to turn airports, and any communities adjacent to them, into hotspots of emissions. Aero engine pollutants are an added concern because, emitted at high altitude, they make a particularly powerful contribution to climate change.

Fuel consumption per passenger mile has been cut by 70 per cent since the dawn of the jet age thanks to larger and sleeker aircraft and to less thirsty engines. More economical turbines account for half this gain. Airlines welcome such efficiency, as much because it saves them money and reduces their exposure to oil price fluctuations, as for its green contribution but is an illustration of how profits and environmental protection can go hand in hand. However there is no gainsaying the statement that, given continuing growth in air travel, reducing the local and global environmental risks of aircraft emissions is a profound challenge.

Economy and pollution prospects: New technologies are in train that offer some prospect that carbon and water vapour emissions can be reduced. Three developments in particular are worth mentioning.

— New communications, navigation and traffic management technologies could enable aircraft to take more direct routes, avoid the waste of stacking and time spent with engines running on the ground.

— New lightweight materials promise both to cut aircraft weight and allow the forming of more aerodynamic wings and fuselages. Modifications such as wing tip extensions can also contribute to economy.

— Replacing fossil fuel is the third possibility. In the longer term hydrogen engines may power radically different aircraft from those of today - an event that America's desire to free itself from dependency on foreign oil may hasten. In the meantime there is scope for using electric fuel cells, already used in unmanned military aircraft, as auxiliary power sources for, say, aircraft equipment and lighting,

Meanwhile the International Civil Aviation Organisation is looking at emissions trading, environmental taxes and other economic instruments because of their promise to more effective in the near future than other forms of regulation or new technologies.

Congestion: Congestion in the air and on the tarmac, because it prolongs engine running, adds to noise and gas emissions and to inefficiency in general. Delays to aircraft can result from:

— Restrictions as ordered by traffic managers on the use of air space

— Lack of runway space and taxiways, or other constraints, on the ground.

— Security controls at aircraft terminals.

Government agencies and aviation regulators are increasingly aware that they, as managers of airports and their associated traffic management systems, have a role in reducing congestion and, with it, environmental impacts. This is leading to the design of air traffic control systems that allow aircraft to fly safely at closer intervals and traverse inhospitable terrain. On the ground better surface radar, mixed-mode operation of parallel runways and techniques that replace the downtime needed to keep runways clear of debris, can all increase the efficiency of operations.

Another useful innovation is the use of Lidar to plot the atmospheric vortices created by large jet engines. This enables the distance between successive aircraft to be reduced. Delays at terminals due to security checks can, likewise, be reduced by technologies that enable passengers to be scanned for hidden weapons while they are walking. Another antidote to the delay of queuing is automatic check-ins. The equipment needed for such procedures is, of course, expensive, but, to the extent that it can get more use from existing terminals may, by postponing the need for airport expansion, bring environmental benefits.

3

Lodging Industry

Hotels are amongst the most visible and important aspects of a country's infrastructure. Hotel industry is a closely linked one to the tourism industry. A number of factors like promotion of tourism and rapid industrial progress have given a boost to hoteliering. The recent liberalisation of trade and opening up of economy will further lead to revolutionary growth in this sector.

With increasing globalisation, career opportunities in this field are not only limited within the country but there are chains of hotels which operate internationally providing scope of a career abroad. It is a glamorous profession which has a bright future. With the growth of hotel industry propelled by foreign and domestic tourism and business travel, the demand for well trained quality personnel too has grown impressively.

The diversity of experience in hotel management is greater than in any other profession. Hotel industry involves combination of various skills like management, food and beverage service, housekeeping, front office operation, sales and marketing, accounting. Today, the rise in corporate activity (leading to greater number of business trips) as well as the wish to travel on holiday has made the hotel industry a very competitive one.

The cost and quality of hotels are usually indicative of the range and type of services available. Due to the enormous increase in tourism worldwide during the last decades of the 20th century, standards, especially those of smaller establishments, have improved considerably. For the sake of greater comparability, rating systems have been introduced, with the one to five stars classification being most common.

Hotel Industry in India has witnessed tremendous boom in recent years. Hotel Industry is inextricably linked to the tourism industry and the growth in the Indian tourism industry has fuelled the growth of Indian hotel industry. The thriving economy and increased business opportunities in India have acted as a boon for Indian hotel industry. The arrival of low cost airlines and the associated price wars have given domestic tourists a host of options. The 'Incredible India' destination campaign and the recently launched 'Atithi Devo Bhavah' (ADB) campaign have also helped in the growth of domestic and international tourism and consequently the hotel industry.

In recent years government has taken several steps to boost travel & tourism which have benefited hotel industry in India. These include the abolishment of the inland air travel tax of 15%; reduction in excise duty on aviation turbine fuel to 8%; and removal of a number of restrictions on outbound chartered flights, including those relating to frequency and size of aircraft. The government's recent decision to treat convention centres as part of core infrastructure, allowing the government to provide critical funding for the large capital investment that may be required has also fuelled the demand for hotel rooms.

The opening up of the aviation industry in India has exciting opportunities for hotel industry as it relies on airlines to transport 80% of international arrivals. The government's decision to substantially upgrade 28 regional airports in smaller towns and privatisation &

expansion of Delhi and Mumbai airport will improve the business prospects of hotel industry in India. Substantial investments in tourism infrastructure are essential for Indian hotel industry to achieve its potential. The upgrading of national highways connecting various parts of India has opened new avenues for the development of budget hotels in India. Taking advantage of this opportunity Tata group and another hotel chain called 'Homotel' have entered this business segment.

Hotel Industry in India currently has supply of 110,000 rooms and there is a shortage of 150,000 rooms fueling hotel room rates across India. According to estimates demand is going to exceed supply by at least 100% over the next 2 years. Five-star hotels in metro cities allot same room, more than once a day to different guests, receiving almost 24-hour rates from both guests against 6-8 hours usage. With demand-supply disparity, hotel rates in India are likely to rise by 25% annually and occupancy by 80%, over the next two years. This will affect the competitiveness of India as a cost-effective tourist destination.

To overcome, this shortage Indian hotel industry is adding about 60,000 quality rooms, currently in different stages of planning and development, which should be ready by 2012. Hotel Industry in India is also set to get a fillip with Delhi hosting 2010 Commonwealth Games. Government has approved 300 hotel projects, nearly half of which are in the luxury range. The future scenario of Indian hotel industry looks extremely rosy. It is expected that the budget and mid-market hotel segment will witness huge growth and expansion while the luxury segment will continue to perform extremely well over the next few years.

Goals and Objectives

In order to carry out its mission, global and departmental goals and objectives, every company shall build a formal structure depicting different hierarchy of management, supervision, and employee (staff) levels. This very structure is refereed to as organisation chart. Moreover, the organisation chart shows reporting relationships span of management, and staff/line functions.

There are two types of relationships that might exist between any two functions at any organisation chart. These are:

— *Solid Lines:* This kind of relationship shows Direct Line Accountability. To illustrate, if position A and B are linked with a solid line, it means (for example) that A shall report to B, that B shall tell A what to do, when to do, and how to it. Lastly, B shall be liable (i.e. responsible) for A.

— *Dotted Lines:* This kind of relationship entitles both positions linked with dotted lines to have a high degree of Cooperation and Communication but not a direct line accountability. Usually in the hotel industry, where the sole aim is to satisfy guests, positions, whatsoever level in the hierarchy they occupy, shall coordinate jointly their efforts so as to provide quality, standard product to their customers. Therefore, examples of dotted lines are numerous in hotel organisation charts.

Every organisation chart shall be flexible, to reflect the ever-changing environmental dynamics and, hence be able to survive. In accordance, organisation charts shall be reviewed periodically in order to determine whether the actual organisation still match the environment needs or not. A SWOT analysis shall be a good start to initiate a change in the organisation chart or not. Last but not least, it is of extreme importance that there are no 2 hotels having exactly the same organisation chart, and that a hotel might have an organisation chart change over time. For, organisation charts shall be tailored to fit the needs of each individual property.

Hotel Characteristics

— All hotels are in the business of renting rooms.

— Hotels vary in size from under 100 rooms to over 5,000.

— Hotels vary in type. They can be center-city hotels, resorts, highway properties, conference centers, and so on.

— Hotels vary in the nature and extent of their facilities. Some hotels offer only rooms, while others have coffee shops, gourmet restaurants, swimming pools, golf courses, and other facilities.

— Hotels vary in the level of service they offer. For example, some offer 24-hour, room service, others offer room service from 7 A.M. to 10 P.M. only, and some do not offer room service at all.

Clearly, hotels are not all alike. No matter what category a hotel falls into, however, it must, be organised in order to:

— coordinate the many specialised tasks and activities necessary to attract and serve guests, and

— produce a reasonable profit consistent with the amount of money and time invested in the enterprise. Organising is, one of the principal jobs of management.

Hotel Organisation Method

Role of Service Departments

To provide lodging to guests, all hotels are organised around four basic functions:

— front desk operation

— housekeeping

— building maintenance/engineering, and

— security.

Beyond these common services, hotels and their departments can vary tremendously. For example, most luxury hotels include a restaurant and beverage department, while most budget facilities do not. The performance of these functions can also vary widely among different types of hotels. Business guests of a convention center may expect hi-tech front desk operations, and guests at a resort may prefer a more personal approach. At any rate, all hotels carry out these functions both behind the scenes and at the front of the house.

Functional Areas

There are two approaches to classify departments in typical hotels:

— Revenue Generating versus Cost Centers: The first approach is trying to differentiate between departments revenue-wise. In fact, this approach entitles that if a department generates revenue to the hotel, it is called a revenue generator. On the other hands, if a department incurs costs without directly contributing to hotel profitability, it is called a cost or support center.

— Front of the House versus Back of House: This approach classifies departments according to department staff's frequency of communication with guests. If communication between staff and guest is frequent, then the department is said to be a front of the house department. On the other hand, if the communication between department staff and guests in nonexistent or on occasions, then the department is said to be back of the house department.

Types of Department

Rooms Division: In a statistics conducted by the U.S. Lodging Industry in 1995, it has been shown that the majority of hotels revenues (60.2 %) is generated from Rooms Division Department under the form of room sales. This very department provides the services guests expect during their stay in the Hotel. Lastly, the Rooms Division Department is typically composed of five different departments:

— Front Office

— Reservation

— Housekeeping

— Uniformed Services

— Telephone

Beneath is a brief description of the different departments decomposing the Rooms Division Department, along with their related main responsibilities:

— Front Office:

  — Sell guestrooms; register guests and design guestrooms

  — Coordinate guest services

  — Provide information

  - — Maintain accurate room statistics, and room key inventories
  - — Maintain guest account statements and complete proper financial settlements

— Reservation:

  - — Receive and process reservation requests for future overnight accommodations.
  - — With technology development, the Reservation Department can, on real time, access the number and types of rooms available, various room rates, and furnishings, along with the various facilities existing in the hotel. There should be close relation-ships with Sales and Marketing Division concerning Large Group Reservations.

— Housekeeping:

  - — Inspects rooms before they are available for sale
  - — Cleans occupied and vacant rooms
  - — Communicates the status of guestrooms to the Front Office Department
  - — Cleans and presses the property's linens, towels, and guest clothing (if equipped to do so, free of charge or for a pre-determined fee)
  - — Maintains recycled and non-recycled inventory items

— Uniformed Services:

  - — *Bell Attendants*: Ensure baggage service between the lobby area and guestrooms
  - — *Door Attendants*: Ensure baggage service and traffic control at hotel entrance(s)
  - — *Valet Parking Attendants*: Ensure parking services for guest's automobiles

  — *Transportation Personnel*: Ensure transportation services for guests from and to the hotel
  — *Concierge*: Assists guests by making restaurant reservations, arranging for transportation, and getting tickets for theater, sporting, or any other special events

— Telephone Department:

— Answers and distributes calls to the appropriate extensions, whether guest, employee, or management extensions

— Places wake-up calls

— Monitors automated systems

— Coordinates emergency communications 'Protects Guest Privacy'

Food & Beverage Department: According to U.S. Lodging 1995 statistics, F&B Department constitutes the second largest revenue generator of a typical hotel with an average of 23.1 for Food sales, and 8.6 % for Beverage sales. In a five-star hotel, Food and Beverage outlets might have the following forms:

— Quick Service

— Table Service

— Speciality Restaurants

— Coffee Shops

— Bars

— Lounges

— Clubs

— Banquets

— Catering Functions - Wedding, Birthdays...

Sales & Marketing Division: A typical hotel should usually have Sales & Marketing division. However, if the staff size, volume business, hotel size, expected group arrivals is low enough, the hotel might have marketing staff placed under the reservation department (i.e. No need for a Sales & Marketing Division). A typical Sales & Marketing Division is composed of four different departments:

— Sales
— Convention Services
— Advertising
— Public Relations

Accounting Division: The Accounting Division monitors the financial activities of the property. Some of the activities that are undertaken in the Accounting Division are listed below:

— Pays outstanding invoices
— Distributes unpaid statements
— Collects amounts owed
— Processes payroll
— Accumulates operating data
— Compiles financial reports
— Makes bank deposits
— Secures cash loans
— Performs other control and processing functions

Engineering and Maintenance Division: This very department maintains the property's structure and grounds as well as electrical and mechanical equipment. Some hotels might have this very division under different names, such as maintenance division, property operation and maintenance department...

Security Division: Security division personnel are usually screened from in house personnel, security officers or retired police officers, across certain physical skills, and prior experience. Some of the functions of the security division are listed below:

— Patrols the property

— Monitors supervision equipment

— Ensures safety and security of guests, visitors, and employees

Human Resources Division: Some of the duties of the human resources division are listed below:

— Responsible for external & internal recruitment

— Calculates employees' salaries, compensation, and tax withholding...

— Administrates employees' paperwork, monitors attendance...

— Maintains good relations with Labour Unions

— Ensures employees' safety and working conditions

Other Divisions: All the above mentioned departments and/or divisions should exist in a typical five-star hotel, however there might be some revenue generators that are specific to certain hotels but not existing in others. Below is a list of some possible extra or other divisions that might exist in a hotel:

— *Retail Outlets*: The revenue earned from this is called a Rental

— *Recreation Facilities*: These facilities may be operated by an independent operator who would pay either a flat fee, a minimum fee and a percentage of the gross receipts or simply a percentage of gross sales. The revenue earned from this is called a Concessions.

— Conference Centers

— Casinos

Hotels may be paid a fee by suppliers that are located

outside the hotel but provide a service to hotel guests e.g. car rentals and photographers.

AMERICANS WITH DISABILITIES ACT (ADA)

Employers also cannot discriminate on the basis of a worker's disabilities. The president's Committee on Employment of the Handicapped estimates that 49 million Americans are disabled in some way, including those with "hidden disabilities" such as learning disabilities, diabetes, illiteracy, and AIDS. Since the passage of the ADA, employers are prohibited from asking job applications about past or current medical conditions. Employers cannot require job applicants to take pre-employment physicals.

In addition, it defines an applicants to be qualified for a job as long as he or she can perform the "essential functions" of the job with or without reasonable accommodation. The term essential functions refer to the job tasks that are fundamental for the performance of the job. For example, as essential function for a bellhop would be the ability to carry heavy luggage or push a full luggage cart. If an individual's disability made this impossible, he or she would not have to be hired.

The employer is required to provide "reasonable accommodations" to make the workplace accessible to the disabled. Reasonable accommodations may include many facilities wheelchair accessible, providing readers or interpreters for those who cannot read or the visually impaired, and modifying or acquiring equipment to allow a disable person to perform essential job functions. The EEOC estimates that about half of the disable require no workplace accommodations in order to perform essential job functions. Of the remaining 50 percent who need accommodations, 20 percent of those accommodations will cost less than $50; and most remaining accommodations will ost less than $500.

Ideal Control Systems

An important part of managing is to measure performance levels and take corrective action if they do not meet the goals of the enterprise. In order to maintain control over all aspects of an organisation, managers and owners must first establish goals against which results can be measured. For example, an organisation may establish a payroll goal of 30 percent of revenues-that is, the operating plan is to spend 30 percent or less of sales on salaries and other payroll expenses. The plan may also provide that a variance of 2 percent is acceptable, but that anything above that is not. If payroll expenses exceed 32 percent, management must take action.

The ideal control system allows managers to quickly recognise and correct deviations from the operating budget (or some other management standard) before they become major problems. One way hotel managers accomplish this is to have accurate forecasting systems. In too many cases, corrections are made long after the problem starts. The longer the period between the variation from property goals and the correction, the weaker the control system and the greater the potential for lost revenue and increased costs. Training plays a key role in control systems. A certain number of errors by front desk personnel and food servers is inevitable-no human system is perfect. But careful training can minimize errors and bring performance levels up to standard.

Many of management's goals can be quantified. The more specific the goal and the easier it is to quantify, the more likely it is that the goal will be met. Guest room occupancy levels, guest counts in restaurants, and revenue and expense targets are examples of quantifiable goals. Not all goals are easy to measure. For example, an operating plan might have a goal of increasing guest satisfaction or employee morale. However, even there it is possible to be more specific and measure the results accordingly. Two of the most important types of controls for hotel managers are financial controls and quality controls.

Financial Control

Among the most useful financial control tools are financial statements. Investors use them to monitor profitability. Lenders view them as measures of financial stability. Managers base their planning on them and monitor the success of their planning with them. In order to understand a hotel financial statement, it is necessary to be familiar with the hotel industry's financial terminology and to understand the manner in which revenues and expenses are grouped by hotel division.

Uniform System of Accounts

In March 1926 the American Hotel & Lodging Association (at that time it was called the American Hotel Association of the United States and Canada) adopted a manual called the Uniform System of Accounts for Hotels. The system was formulated by a committee of accountants and hoteliers in New York City. The ninth edition bore a new title to better encompass all segments of the industry: The Uniform System of Accounts for the Lodging Industry.

The Uniform System of Accounts for the Lodging Industry classifies the different types of hotel revenues and expenses, and groups them in the statement of income by division or department. The statement of income is one of management's major control tools. It shows the total sales by product or service category (rooms, food, beverage, and so on) for a stated period of time, the expenses incurred in generating those sales, and the profit earned or the loss incurred as a result of those activities.

There are three types of hotel expenses: divisional expenses, overhead expenses, and fixed charges or capital costs. Divisional expenses include a wide range of items, such as rooms division payroll expenses, restaurant laundry, and telephone supplies like message pads and pencils. Overhead expenses are costs such as marketing and energy-costs that relate to the entire hotel and not to one specific division. Fixed charges or capital costs are expenses related to the investment, such as insurance on the building and contents, and interest on the mortgage loan.

The uniform system also classifies assets (something of value that is owned) and liabilities (what is owed to creditors). Examples of assets might be the hotel building itself, furniture and equipment, and courtesy vans to transport guests to and from airports. Liabilities include items such as the mortgage loan and food purchases for which payment is due. All of these items are grouped together in the financial statement known as the balance sheet. A balance sheet reports the financial position of a business by presenting its assets, liabilities, and owner's or shareholders' equity on a given date.

Quality Controls

It is a relatively simple task to standardise the quality and cost of a manufactured product. This is because products, whether they be toasters or skis, are produced in a factory under strictly controlled 'conditions. Some assembly lines are computerised, and many use robots to perform some functions. Moreover, quality control inspectors not, only monitor all operations but can inspect each finished item before it leaves the plant and a consumer purchases it.

Service businesses such as hotels operate under an entirely different set of circumstances. The "product" that a hotel produces-the experience of staying there is manufactured in the hotel "factory" right in front of the consumer. For example, a guest enters a hotel, goes into the lounge, sits down at a table, and orders a strawberry daiquiri.

The product in this case is not simply the daiquiri-it also includes the lounge, the server, and the bartender who mixes the drink. It is this total experience that the guest pays for. If the guest had just wanted a strawberry daiquiri, he or she could have made one at home or bought a bottled one at the corner liquor store. Because of the nature of a service business, it is extremely difficult to standardise or even control the service that guests receive. There are too many variables that can interfere with the process-including the guests, who, for example, may be rude and provoke employees to be rude in return.

Opportunities for dissatisfaction abound. Take our guest who ordered the strawberry daiquiri. Possibly the guest had to wait for a table because none was available or the host was out of the room temporarily. Maybe the seating was prompt, but the guest had to wait longer than expected for the order because the ice machine or the drink mixer was broken. Perhaps the bartender was preoccupied with a personal problem instead of concentrating on fixing a perfect strawberry daiquiri. Even if everything else goes well, it can all be spoiled if the guest, has to wait too long for the check or if there is a mistake on it.

All of these possibilities exist whenever a guest enters the lounge. Any of them can affect the quality of the experience (the product) and thus the guest's perception of the lounge and the hotel. This one transaction is a single example of the many kinds of things that can go wrong in a hotel that is open 24 hours a day, seven days a week, where guests interact regularly with, and receive service from, front desk agents, food servers, room attendants, bell persons, concierges, valets, maintenance people, and gift shop employees.

Product and service consistency is of primary importance and can only be achieved through quality controls such as:

— Setting standards that answer the needs and expectations of guests

— Selecting employees who are capable of achieving those standards and who are motivated to do so · Conducting continual training and certification programmes for all employees at every level

— Involving employees in structuring job descriptions, setting performance, standards, and solving work problems

— Having a feedback system so that all managers and employees know they are achieving what they have set out to do-satisfy the guest

— Rewarding managers and employees for achieving quality goals

Quality programmes at hotels go by various names: "quality assurance" (QA) and "total quality management" (TQM) are two examples. Although their names vary, the goal of all such programmes is to provide quality service to guests.

Setting standards

Quality is an overriding concern in the hotel industry, but what does "quality" mean? There is no universal industry agreement on what quality is, nor should there be. Quality has to do with guest expectations versus reality. When guests check into a $40-a-night budget hotel, they expect a certain standard of service and no more. If they get what they expect (or a little more), they have enjoyed a quality experience from their point of view. If they get less than what they expect or they were paying for, then they will think they received poor-quality service. The formula is the same for a hotel room that costs $250 a night. A guest who pays that amount has certain expectations. His or her perception of quality depends to a large degree on whether those expectations are met or exceeded.

Most hotels strive for quality for their type of product and target market. Quality, then, means that the guest experience-in terms of the cleanliness of the rooms, the taste and presentation of the food, and the physical condition of the hotel-is consistent with what the management has promised and is trying to deliver. Some lodging chains that emphasize food and offer the same menu at all of their units go to great lengths to ensure that food quality will be the same at every unit, because that is what their repeat visitors expect. Club Med is one example:

> The buffets at each and every Club Med are a veritable catalogue of traditional French cuisine: pungent cheeses, freshly baked baguettes and croissants, pates and terrines, crudites, ratatouille, cote d' agneau, quiche, coulibiac, even frogs legs To add a touch of the indigenously exotic, local specialties account for at least five percent of each club's menu.

The Ritz-Carlton Hotel Company also sets very high standards. According to the management of the Ritz-Carlton chain, "Customer satisfaction is a deeply held belief at the Ritz-Carlton and begins with an absolute understanding of the needs and expectations of our customer." The chain achieves this understanding by forming focus groups of Ritz-Carlton current and prospective guests and by recording guest preferences that are detected and reported by all front-line employees. This information is used to set guest-service standards.

To achieve quality standards, hotel managers-with the help of individual employees and" quality teams" formed from hotel personnel-must create procedures for hotel staff to follow. For example, when a room attendant has finished cleaning a guestroom, the position of the furniture, the number of towels and other guest amenities, and-most important-the overall cleanliness of the room must be exactly the same every day for every room. How many towels to leave in the bathroom or what constitutes "clean" should not be left to the discretion of the person doing the cleaning.

Procedures must be established for each task to be performed. At the same time, a standard of what is acceptable and what is not must be spelled out for each procedure. It is not reasonable to set standards without specifically detailing the procedures that must be followed in order to achieve those standards.

The following example of a food service procedure and standard concerns the task of greeting guests at a table:

> *Procedure*: After table is seated, greet the guest(s): "Good morning. May I offer you some coffee?" Be pleasant, unhurried. Pour coffee with cup on table, and to right of guest-If tea is served, the tea pot is served on a butter plate with a doily, lemon on top of tea pot.
>
> *Standard*: Make the guest feel comfortable. Strike a positive note in your "beginning" with the guest.

Selecting employees

Ritz-Carlton emphasizes the importance of employee selection in its quality management programme. Ritz-Carlton's managers have devised a highly sophisticated predictive instrument, using superior employees as benchmarks, that allows them to determine whether the candidates for a specific position are capable of living up to the chain's service standards.

Training employees

It is not enough for a hotel to establish standards and procedures and select employees to carry them out. Employees must be shown how to perform the procedures. Employees who have never cleaned a guestroom or waited on a table can't be expected to know what to do simply because they've been given a manual.

To succeed, training must be ongoing and have the full commitment of management. At Ritz-Carlton, all hotels have a director of human resources on staff who is assisted by the hotel's quality leader, who acts as an advisor. Each work area has a departmental trainer who is charged with the training and certification of new employees in that area. According to Horst Schulze, current vice chairman and former president and CEO of Ritz-Carlton, " At the Ritz- Carlton, it is everybody's job, daily, to make our people more valuable."

Involving employees

All successful quality programmes use a participative style of management. Judy King, owner and president of Quality Management Services, lists basic beliefs in employee involvement in problem-solving:

— The person doing the job knows how the job can be done better.

— Problem-solving and decision-making should be done at the lowest capable level in the organisation.

— People are the greatest untapped resource in the organisation.

— People will meet expectations if they have been enabled to do so and, with encouragement, will exceed them.

Ritz-Carlton employees are expected and empowered to solve problems. On the Ritz-Carlton "Gold Standards" card that every employee carries, it says, "Any employee who receives a customer complaint' owns' the complaint." Employees are encouraged to break out of their regular routine and solve guest problems immediately and ensure that they do not recur. Teams of workers from different divisions are often put together to resolve conflicts between internal operation problems and external guest expectations.

Evaluating quality programmes

Management must verify the consistency of product and service quality in order to evaluate the success of its quality efforts. Ritz-Carlton, for example, depends heavily on real-time reports, called "guest incident action forms," that are generated daily by employees. These reports are analysed and quickly acted on so that incidents of guest dissatisfaction will not be repeated.

One of the simplest ways to evaluate the quality of an operation is called "management by walking around." Successful hotel managers have found that taking periodic tours of the hotel and staying alert to what is going on around them is one of the best ways of ensuring that the quality programme is working. There is a saying in the United States Navy that also applies to the hotel business: "You get what you inspect, not what you expect."

Guest comment cards are also important evaluation tools. Although many managers feel these cards encourage negative comments, they are nevertheless valuable. Cards typically are placed in guestrooms on the dresser or desk. Some hotels require front desk agents to ask departing guests if they have completed a card. Experience has shown that open-ended questions that ask guests to write a description of their experiences do not work as well as simple rating scales, where guests can indicate their level of satisfaction with various components of the hotel's service and facilities. There should be room on the card, however, for guests to add comments if they choose and to identify employees whom they wish to single out either positively or negatively.

Another evaluation method involves hiring outside inspectors, usually referred to as "mystery shoppers." These inspectors, who are not known to hotel employees, make reservations, stay in a guestroom, eat in the dining room, check out, and then prepare elaborate reports on the level of service they received. Some hotels announce inspections in advance and the inspectors are known. While employees often favour this system, the level of management confidence in the results of such inspections tends to be much lower.

Hotel Organisation of the Future

No hotel company operating today can be unaware of the swift pace of global change and its impact on every facet of the hospitality industry. With just five years left in this century, we can expect change to be the only constant. New business practices are evolving virtually as fast as our technologies, while resistance to change has become one of the primary causes of business failure.

The specter of constant change raises fundamental questions as to the creation of shareholder wealth in a capital-constrained, highly competitive environment. How will hotel organisations build shareholder wealth, and what key drivers will result in success? What future products and services will be essential in a technology-driven, global environment marked by rising customer expectations? Moreover, what alternative approaches and skills must organisations develop to ensure market success?

The future success of hotel organisations will be driven in large part by the ability to foresee — and capitalise — on change. Beyond this truism, however, there is an urgent need to identify what will be required in the competitive environment of the future with its intense focus on serving customer needs. The hospitality industry — as is the case with business generally — is subject to deep currents of change set in motion as economic and social systems shaped in the industrial era evolve to a knowledge-based era driven by technology advances.

In this period of global transition, it behooves hotel organisations to examine the key factors that will not only define success, but the ability to survive in coming years. Many of these issues were spotlighted in a global study undertaken by the Economist Intelligence Unit and co-sponsored by Arthur Andersen. The Successful Corporation of the Year 2000 surveyed more than 600 senior executives around the world. Its mission was to identify the characteristics needed to lead successful businesses in the next century. These executives offer a number of compelling messages regarding the key success factors of the future.

Customers will have the strongest influence on the corporation in the year 2000. Indeed, these executives believe that the customer will be "king" in the new century. Exceptional leadership was by far the attribute most frequently cited by CEOs and senior executives; the consensus appears to be that successful companies in the year 2000 will be led by corporate visionaries. A strategic planning focus is not only essential, but must embody a concept of planning for the future that anticipates change, rather than being based exclusively on historical models. In structuring organisations for the future, companies must build management capabilities to deal with one of the most critical challenges — diversity in the marketplace. Employing information technology to drive business success in this information-driven era is not only the path of least resistance, but vital to virtually every aspect of operations.

The study's top-line results create an excellent backdrop to address key issues confronting the hotel industry, and what factors will lead to membership — rather than rejection — in the elite club of the world's corporate success stories in the year 2000.

From an Asset to Customer Focus

Recognising that the hotel industry has a somewhat split personality reflecting the inherent conflicts between its real estate and operational aspects, it is important to understand the industry's real estate origins and how they are shaping the challenges ahead.

The origins of the industry's real estate persona are embodied in the classic theory of location - "if we build it, they will come." As a result of this "building" complex, the industry has tended to have a real estate and asset orientation, rather than a customer focus. From the hotel company perspective — especially that of the brand-oriented "chain" — the varied interests of a diffused property ownership group can be quite different than the singular interest of the chain that operates and markets the properties.

Even when the ownership of geographically dispersed hotel properties is controlled by a single hotel organisation, the financial structuring tends to be property-specific. Corporate financial strategies are frequently subjugated to the needs of the last property deal brought into the company's fold. Each property in a so-called "chain," is frequently the subject of a unique and distinctive ownership and financial structure. This phenomenon — quite common in the real estate sector, but unusual for business enterprises generally — makes for elusive economies of scale in the structuring and financing of property-driven expansion.

Collectively, these factors have produced low comparative returns in real estate, although criticism levelled at commercial real estate returns is somewhat less germane to the hotel industry, where management and franchise fees can produce high returns for those companies where property ownership is held by third parties. Nevertheless, average returns in the real estate industry in the United States, for example, are just over 10 percent, compared to small company stock returns at almost 20 percent and large company stocks at an average of about 15 percent.

While hotel chains have adopted traditional corporate frameworks, there are a number of predominantly real estate-driven, family-owned businesses in the hotel sector that continue to operate as relatively unstructured organisations. In meeting the future, these businesses will need plans, people and processes in order to establish viable corporate forms that can compete in tomorrow's marketplace and capitalise upon its opportunities.

In today's changed environment, the hotel organisation must deal with a number of new realities. Investors in our industry are no longer satisfied with long-term capital appreciation and psychic income that heretofore were often the justification for otherwise seemingly uneconomic investments in hotel property or, indeed, hotel chains. The first reality is that there is a very specific and identifiable relationship between bottom line performance and value. Improvements in business operations raises values. It is not surprising, therefore, that the new owners attracted to this industry in recent years have new sets of demands. This transformation from an old-guard group of investors and owners to income and return-driven newcomers has meant that the once "quiet enjoyment" of operators in their management of hotels for third parties is being disturbed, interrupted and overturned.

These challenges all take place in an environment where capital has become extremely selective in markets that have little stability. A global shortage of capital will not remain a short-term problem, and future hotel organisations must have a stronger alignment to capital providers — a critical "customer" group. Hotel companies will need to compete by offering better returns and performance than in the past. Hotel chains have found their development timetables quashed in recent years, making it difficult to achieve goals of critical mass often required to improve performance. These factors are driving consolidation in the brand "sweepstakes." Capital markets, therefore, continue to favour well-established companies, a reality that must drive entrepreneurial organisations to meet the future now by planning for an evolving corporate context in which to operate.

Key Success Factors

Within this broad context, hotel developers, owners and management companies will all need to develop new strategies, skills and processes that look forward to the competitive demands of the future. These ultimately must address issues related to vision and planning, as well as organisational skill sets and processes to attract and retain customers. To stake a claim in the future, current business practices should be examined in light of what can be expected to be the key success factors in the year 2000.

Embrace a global change orientation. As the information age produces greater worldwide integration of business activities, a global knowledge base will become invaluable. Success in local and regional hotel markets will be shaped decisively by a global business environment that defines capital movement, customer expectations and applications of new technologies.

Focus on the Customer. If the customer is "king" in the 21st century, hotel organisations will be best served by focusing less on their hotel assets as measures of success, and more on their customers. This involves a fundamental shift in viewing the real estate asset as the wealth creator — to the customer as the key to building shareholder wealth. A customer focus must imbue business decisions at all levels of developing and operating a hotel organisation. Pursuing such a course will inevitably impact shareholder wealth. To accomplish this, however, customers need to participate in the product development process.

Fully realising a customer focus in the industry poses a significant challenge. The hotel industry must confront problems due to conflicts between operational needs and real estate goals. Quite simply, an operator must remain customer-focused, but the short-term strategies to meet these needs may be inconsistent with the long-term objectives of property owners. Balancing those goals will be essential. A customer focus implies a significant shift in what drives hotel development — placing primary emphasis on the customer with the locations to follow. Nevertheless, a hotel organisation with its large investment in fixed assets — the real estate — can never be as nimble as a consumer products company in adjusting products and services to match rapid shifts in the marketplace.

The Japanese taught us that the concept of "zero defects" in products and services can yield tremendous benefits. But today an even more rigorous standard dominates — quality that surprises. In practical terms, the hotel industry finds it extremely difficult to meet the standard of zero defects in service. Hotel services are based primarily on people, not computers or other equipment. Quality that surprises takes the concept of zero defects a step further.

Yesterday's surprising product or service is today's status quo. Twenty years ago, a business executive did not expect a consistent and predictable level of service wherever he or she travelled in the world. Today that is a standard — not the exception — as is the expectation for sophisticated technology in hotel rooms to support business needs. With customer discrimination so acute, it is not surprising that brand loyalty is a diminishing "commodity" in the hotel industry.

Find the ingredients for visionary leadership. Today's hotel organisations need to recognise the need for visionary leadership. The ability to forecast the future — to anticipate change rather than react to it — will be one of the single greatest determinants of market dominance in the years ahead. The old "command and control" model of leadership is giving way to a focus on leadership in ideas, information, inspiration, vision and teamwork. Warren Bennis, an authority on leadership in the U.S., puts it this way — "For the most part, failing organisations tend to be over-managed and under-led. The leader sets the tone for the moral character, the vision, the corporate culture and the fiber of the institution."

While visionary leadership is essential, it must be linked to business operations and foster a risk bias, rather than a procedural bias. This will allow the organisation to stretch and, in turn, change. And it must be shared by empowered professionals and staff throughout the organisation, including those who meet the customer.

Overcoming the resistance to change can be a daunting task, particularly in large hotel organisations in which diversions from the status quo may threaten established management lines. It suggests that a culture based on conformance may need to be replaced by an emphasis on flexibility, learning and cooperation. Management competencies will need to be aligned in order to achieve the desired result. For many organisations, this may mean a shift from traditional hierarchies typical of companies in an industrial era to a flatter organisation with a more transparent interface between leadership, organisational functions and employees.

Create a defensible position through corporate strategy. For many of the industry's leaders, vision is driven by the strategic planning process, a function which has become critical for success. Strategic planning, however, has at times been a step-child in the hotel industry, and it is often the first to be cut when organisations are downsized. It is clearly in transition. There also has been a tendency to decentralise and simplify this function — both actions of potential benefit. Strategic planning must be led by the top people in the organisation — the CEO and COO. On the other hand, it should be close enough to the customer to ensure that planners can "listen" to and be influenced by customer needs.

Empower Management. Beyond the ability to envision the future, core management capabilities will make the difference — they are essential. A clear vision without the management skills to support it cannot be a recipe for success. First and foremost, hotel management must have strategic development skills and the ability to integrate complex factors affecting success. Market volatility has become the norm, in part caused by the rapidly changing tastes of customers. Customers are increasingly approaching the hotel industry with widely different social, economic and political backgrounds, to say nothing of employees. Being able to deal with these diversities in a positive and constructive fashion that capitalises on the differences, rather than working to find ways to mitigate them, is the clear path for successful management in the future.

The organisation will also need to be imbued with a sense of entrepreneurship that reacts proactively to the market's diversity. Traditional organisations that follow well documented rules must give way to leaders who can balance a sense of discipline with that of flexibility. Talent and resources must be marshalled and leveraged.

In an industry with high fixed costs and labour intensity, the concept of leverage in the hotel business is an all-important one. Improving labour productivity through technology must be a goal for today's forward-looking hotel organisation. Management must also be able to narrow the gap between the employer and the employee, forcing a flatter organisation in the process. This will put management closer to the customer and speed the two-way communication process up and down the organisation.

Be in the information fast lane. The traditional role of information technology (IT) as a back office support for accounting and bookkeeping has clearly moved front and center stage. IT today influences all aspects of business from corporate strategies to organisational structure — and from the very business processes it is designed to support to performance measurement. In a world where the customer is "king," IT must also deliver in two critical areas: sales and marketing and customer service.

Technology was once viewed as a way to reduce costs by replacing people. That attitude has been firmly supplanted by one that seeks IT support for the creative work that all organisations must pursue. IT must allow organisations to react more speedily to market needs and, of course, produce the fulfilment of customer demands both quickly and accurately. To do this IT must operate on a decentralised basis. IT delivers, but it has to be the right information to the right people, and it needs to be done on a timely basis.

4

Restaurant Industry

The restaurant industry runs the gamut from gourmet restaurants to hot dog stands. The National Restaurant Association (NRA) estimates that in the year 2001 food service sales will be $399 billion, and the industry will employ 11.3 million people in 844,000 establishments. Restaurant industry sales equal more than four percent of the U.S. gross domestic product. The percentage of the food dollar spent away from home is 45.8 percent and is expected to reach 53 percent by 2010. More than 54 billion meals are eaten in restaurants, schools, and work cafeterias each year. The most popular ethnic cuisines are Italian, Chinese, and Mexican.

Types of Facilities and Markets

The restaurant industry includes many different types of facilities and markets. For reporting and other purposes, the industry can be divided into the following segments:

— Eating and drinking places
— Lodging operations
— Transportation market
— Recreational market
— Business and industry market

— Educational market
— Health care market
— Retail market
— Corrections food service
— Military food service
— Contractors

Industry Development

Social and economic trends have emerged to shape the restaurant industry. The most profound trend is the working woman. With a larger income, women view restaurants not only as an affordable way to dine, but also as a convenience for themselves and their family. Restaurants provide an alternative to the added stress of arriving home from the office and dropping everything to cook the family's evening meal. The increase in household incomes has created a desire and convenience for people to spend time dining away from home or ordering takeout meals. The association cites households with a pretax income of $30,000 or more spends a larger amount of time dining out.

In short, the increase in working women has created a larger household income in which people can afford to eat away from home. The mere convenience of avoiding a night of cooking over the stove after a long day at the office is enticing to many women and their families. This trend is expected to remain long-term as people's lives continue on a fast-paced schedule. Whether it's driving a son or daughter to a school function or staying late at the office, sitting down at home for a meal with the entire family is hard to come by.

From a promotional products perspective, understanding the driving forces behind the changes in the restaurant industry will enable eatery owners to properly target the audience they decide to pursue. The restaurant industry has two distinct audience segments: full- and limited-service operations. Both segments attract a certain clientele as well as various promotional products.

Full-Service and Limited-Service

The full-service segment of the restaurant industry can be categorised as sit-down restaurants that cater to the customer with a sense of personal attention. For example, an Italian restaurant with a hostess, a choice of wines and Italian music playing softly in the background is a full-service experience. Many full-service restaurants are competing for customers, not only in the full-service market, but with the fast-food or limited-service segment of the industry as well.

According to one generally accepted definition, full-service restaurants are restaurants that:

— Feature a dozen or more main-course items on the menu, and

— Cook to order

Full-service restaurants are generally categorised in terms of price, menu, or atmosphere.

Price

When the focus is on price, restaurants can be categorised as luxury, highpriced, mid-priced, or low-priced establishments.

Menu

Restaurants such as steak houses and seafood restaurants

are full service restaurants defined in terms of menu. For example, Outback Steakhouse specialises in beef; Red Lobster features shrimp, crab, and lobster on its menu.

Ethnic restaurants feature a specific cuisine as their distinctive theme. Romano's Macaroni Grill features Italian food, for example. Other ethnic restaurants serve Chinese, Greek, Japanese, Polynesian, Scandinavian, Korean, or Indian food, to name a few.

Atmosphere

Some restaurants are known primarily for their atmosphere that is, for their unique architecture, decor, and / or setting. Show business and sports motifs-currently very fashionable in the industry-provide themes for a growing number of popular restaurants. The Hard Rock Cafe chain, which started in London and now has restaurants in major cities around the world, features Elvis Presley, the Beatles, and other rock-star music memorabilia.

Other categories: Full-service restaurants can be categorised in other ways besides price, menu, or atmosphere. For example, there are dinner houses. Dinner houses are distinguishable by their combination of decor, informal atmosphere, and eclectic menus that draw from ethnic and traditional offerings. Many consider Steak and Ale and Bennigan's founder Norman Brinker the father of this restaurant class. He also operated Chili's Grill & Bar, Romano's Macaroni Grill, and others. Almost all dinner houses are chain-affiliated. Olive Garden, T.G.I. Friday's, and Ruby Tuesday are all casual dinner houses, one of the largest segments within the full-service category

Family restaurants: Another mainstay in the full-service restaurant category-cater to families, with an emphasis on satisfying the needs of children. Family restaurants serve breakfast, lunch, and dinner, offering traditional menu items. Their pricing falls between casual dinner houses and quick-service restaurants. A major source of revenue for some family restaurants-such as Cracker Barrel - is an on-site gift shop.

To compete against its market segment as well as other establishments, the fullservice restaurant prides itself on customer appreciation. To survive, full-service restaurants must have a loyal customer following. This is accomplished by offering unique menu choices and a creative atmosphere that will entice the customer not only to return, but also to inform his or her acquaintances of the establishment. The biggest challenge for full-service operators is to attract customers, then maintain their loyalty.

The 90s brought the theme restaurants. These include restaurants catering to music, movies, sports or environmental enthusiasts. Many theme establishments have the advertising and physical appearance to draw customers from all walks of life. Many are tourists who want an opportunity to view memorabilia and catch a glimpse of the creative interior that mirrors the establishment's theme.

Most full-service restaurants, especially theme establishments, will include logoed merchandise as a method of advertising. Customers will find T-shirts and a host of other items with a restaurant's logo on them. These items play an important role in earning customer loyalty and promoting the name of the establishment. Distributors have an advantage servicing the restaurant industry because they simply need to walk inside an establishment to get a hint of its decor and customer base, thus receiving a better idea as to what promotional products would be most appealing to the customers.

On the other end of the scale, limited-service restaurants cater to a much fasterpaced clientele. With corporate downsizing, employees are working longer hours and having meals ordered at the workplace. Longer hours and lack of time have transformed family mealtime into "home meal replacement." Fast-food restaurants and delis offer convenient alternatives to people on the go. The drive-up window has replaced the dining room in many limited-service establishments.

A trend within the limited-service segment is the emergence of carryout services within grocery stores, retail stores, bookstores and gasoline convenience stores. The National Restaurant Association states that nearly 30 percent of all retail establishments are eating and drinking places. Both the retail and bookstore markets are incorporating food services as a marketing tool to keep customers in the stores longer. The grocery stores already have used food to entice its customers to stay and shop; however, many customers will purchase a carryout meal to avoid preparing a meal when they get home.

Gasoline convenience stores are growing tremendously because of the possibility for additional revenue from drivers travelling on a trip or returning home from work. Many are building in residential areas in order to be easily accessible to nearby residents. The limited-service segment opens many doors to food-on-the-go suppliers who are interested in testing unique products specifically designed for the customer on the move. With intense competition between limited-service establishments, owners must rely on creative ideas to separate themselves from the rest of the competition. For example, a product that fits in the automobile to serve as a reminder to visit a convenience store for gasoline and sandwiches is a marketing tool appropriate for people whose car has taken the place of the kitchen table.

With thousands of restaurants to choose from, distributors must understand the establishment, its clientele and the competition to offer promotional products that will make a lasting impact. Whether it is full- or limited-service establishments, there are differences in the needs of restaurants within these segments. What works for the Italian restaurant may not work for the Mexican restaurant down the street. Promotional products are heavily based on customer demand or the usefulness of the product for the market's customers.

Full-Service Success

Two full-service restaurants that have survived the times and made a lasting name for themselves both nationally and worldwide are Ithaca, New York-based Moosewood Restaurant and Driftwood, Texas-based The Salt Lick. Despite outside competition and slow seasons, both restaurants have retained customer loyalty by listening to the needs of its customers. With a combined 55 years in business, Moosewood Restaurant and The Salt Lick understand the importance of customer appreciation. The Moosewood Restaurant is a vegetarian restaurant established in 1973 at a time when people were asking themselves if they could eat just vegetables. Situated in the same spot in Ithaca, New York, the restaurant has undergone several design changes over the years. Ned Asta, a collective member for 20 years, says the restaurant's logo also has undergone several changes.

"The first logo included a moose under a tree with the name Moosewood Restaurant underneath it," says Asta. "Later, Ithaca, New York was added to the logo to promote the location as well as the restaurant. Then 11 years ago, the restaurant was being featured in Bon

Appetite magazine, so I designed the third logo. It featured three moose with a spectrum of blended colours behind them. The logo says Moosewood Restaurant on the top of the logo with Ithaca, New York on the bottom. The restaurant wanted to sell T-shirts in the back of the magazine, so the staff decided to take advantage of the situation by having a new logo designed."

The real attraction to the restaurant, however, is Moosewood's cookbooks. The first book was published 24 years ago and more have appeared every couple of years. Each cookbook focuses on a specific food category. For example, the book due out this year is on soups and salads, last year's book focused on desserts and another is called Sundays At Moosewood that centers on the restaurant's ethnic day dishes that are served every Sunday.

"I believe the cookbooks attract customers to the restaurant and also carry the restaurant," says Asta. "The attraction to the restaurant began with the original book that came out in 1973 when the idea of a vegetarian lifestyle emerged. The timing was very good, and the book became one of the best-sellers nationwide. The name of the first cookbook that came out simply was called The Moosewood Cookbook. The restaurant has followed up on the success of the book by publishing several more throughout the years. Every new book has the name Moosewood Restaurant on it with the original logo on the back."

In Driftwood, Texas, The Salt Lick has a success story of its own. Established in 1969 by the late Thurman Roberts, The Salt Lick came into existence after friends encouraged Thurman and his wife Hisako to open their own restaurant incorporating the many barbecue recipes that had been handed down from generation to generation. Bridgett Duncan, office assistant at The Salt Lick, says the restaurant is a rustic, down home, good time family barbecue place.

"The restaurant has changed significantly since its beginnings in 1969," says Duncan. "The Salt Lick started out as just an outdoor barbecue pit where people would come and get their food off the pit, go sit down someplace and eat it. Benches were then brought in for patrons to sit on. The area with the benches eventually became enclosed and is now known as our porch. The rest of the building was built inward, so there was not one main building. It wasn't too long after that when floors were added to replace the sawdust material. The Salt Lick is a place where people can come, let their hair down and have a good time."

She says the restaurant has one of the few open pit barbecues left in central Texas. However, its international appeal is in the sauce. People from around the world have ordered The Salt Lick's Sauce Gift Pack and Salt Lick Sauce Half Case for its three famous barbecue sauces including Famous Secret Recipe BBQ, The Best Dry Rub and Lauren's Habanero BBQ Sauce.

"Our sauce is world renowned with people calling from all over to have a bottle," says Duncan. "It's only available through the restaurant or our mail order catalogue."

Full-Scale Merchandise

What is interesting about the successes of the Moosewood Restaurant and The Salt Lick is the creative uses of cookbooks and barbecue sauce to promote the restaurant on a grand scale. While it may not have been apparent to the establishments at the time, the cookbooks and sauce were innovative promotional products that continue to generate revenue for the restaurants more than 20 years after their inception. Several years later, both establishments have incorporated common-day promotional items to promote themselves.

Asta says the Moosewood Restaurant originally started with T-shirts it wanted to feature in an advertisement of a magazine the restaurant was appearing in. The Tshirts then evolved into white linen aprons with the logo on them and nightshirts with the slogan "I Dream of Moosewood." The restaurant eventually started offering baseball caps, mugs and bumper stickers with the slogan "Eat Your Vegetables"-

Moosewood restaurant

"One of the latest products we have are linen tote bags," says Asta. "People use them when they go to the market to put their vegetables in. We want good quality products that will last a long time. For that reason, all of our shirts, aprons and hats are made of cotton."

As a marketing strategy last December, Asta created a merchandise window to promote Moosewood's logoed products. She says a large moose replica was positioned at a window in the restaurant's new bar cafe. With the help of snow, candy canes and a large moose, all the products were displayed so the public could see what merchandise was available inside the restaurant. The window display was successful in selling the restaurant's merchandise for Christmas.

Asta says while the merchandise is popular for customers, the complimentary brochure and postcards are equally attractive. The black and white postcards feature the slogan "I Lick My Plate Clean at Moosewood Restaurant." The brochure is appealing to customers because it includes a history about the restaurant, where it is located, what the restaurant caters to, who works there as well as pictures of all the cookbooks the restaurant has published.

"After the cookbooks came out, people started saying that we were famous and asked if we had any matchbooks or something they could take with them," says Asta. "We came up with the idea of free postcards and those were well received. The Tshirts are our biggest sellers because the tourist market is June through September, so travellers will purchase T-shirts or order them over the phone when they arrive home. The restaurant also created a 10- and 25-year anniversary shirt." Similar to Moosewood Restaurant, The Salt Lick started offering promotional merchandise because of customer demand. Duncan says the establishment offers a variety of T-shirts, baseball caps, sweatshirts and cups. The caps and a few T-shirts include a logo with the slogan "Ultimate Barbecue Cuisine." Many customers will take a complimentary mail order catalogue that features all the merchandise and sauce available through the restaurant as well as a menu that describes how The Salt Lick was established.

"The restaurant started offering merchandise because we wanted to cater to the customer," says Duncan. "Customers wanted to have our sauce at home, so that was one of the first things we started. The T-shirts arrived after people wanted something as a memory of the restaurant. The response from our merchandise has been absolutely incredible. It seems like everybody wants to wear The Salt Lick T-shirt with pride." Duncan adds that the restaurant has not expanded into other products because it is not as concerned with the marketing aspect as it is with making good barbecue. The products that are available are what customers have demanded.

Limited Time and Limited-Service

People often find themselves with several things to do and not enough time to do them. It is for this segment of the population that limited-service restaurants were created. Whether it is a fast-food chain, coffeehouse or stop-and-go, the limitedservice establishment is providing customers with a demanding convenience. The National Restaurant Association indicates that one out of five takeout food consumers is a daily user. Those customers represent half of all takeout occasions. Major growth in quick-service restaurants continues to come from hamburger chains as well as chicken, sandwich, and Mexican-food chains. Much of the growth is outside the United States.

The type or number of menu items alone does not determine the winners. A commitment to good service and providing nutritional menu choices has taken center stage. McDonald's now guarantees hot food; fast, friendly service; and double-check drive-thru accuracy. A survey of 27 restaurant chains-including 19 quick-service chains-with 50,000 outlets found that at least three-quarters of them offered menu choices for health-conscious consumers. Examples included low-fat milk, skinless chicken, and reduced or low-calorie salad dressing. Nine out of ten chains said they used vegetable fats instead of animal fats for frying.

While a limited-service establishment may not have all the personal touches of a full-service restaurant, there is a loyalty among limited-service customers that promotional products can reach. With intense competition emerging between limitedservice establishments, it is becoming increasingly important to maintain a loyal customer base. An important method of accomplishing that is incorporating promotional products into the customers' orders.

For fast-food restaurants such as McDonald's and Burger King, children have enjoyed kid's meals that include plastic toys depicting the establishment's mascots. Coffeehouses have used creative ideas such as cooking a muffin in a logoed coffee mug that the customer keeps for refills during repeat visits. Other limited-service establishments include logoed T-shirts, matchbooks, coasters, magnets and buttons. Many of these items are complimentary to the customer as a reminder of the establishment.

The limited-service market has many opportunities for promotional products. The National Restaurant Association notes that in an average month 78 percent of U.S. households use some form of carryout or delivery. It is obvious that the limitedservice market has a large audience that can be reached via promotional products. For example, ast-food restaurants have been offering logoed glasses and toys to customers for many years. Promotional products are an inexpensive medium that limited-service establishments can utilise to promote their name and logo to the public.

The full-service market is custom-oriented; therefore, it is essential that distributors create a promotion that leaves a sense of appreciation in the customer. Full-service establishments want and need customers to return and a well-crafted promotional product could be the difference between a high turnover or a loyal customer base.

The limited-service market works in a similar manner. Although limited service establishments need customers, the focus is to create name and logo recognition to a mass audience. With millions of people who enjoy hamburgers, limited-service operators must separate themselves from the rest of the competition that sells hamburgers. To accomplish this, promotional products with a relatively low cost and function can create long-term exposure to a large audience.

Lodging operations

Food service outlets in lodging operations range from gourmet restaurants to coffee shops and even quick-service outlets. Lodging food service sales are tremendous. In 1999, Marriott Hotels and Resorts alone had food sales of $1.65 billion. Food sales for the top eight hotel chains totalled $5.7 billion.

Transportation market

Travellers eat at highway stops; on airplanes, ships, and trains; at airport terminals and train stations; and at other facilities in the transportation market-a market that enjoys about $3.7 billion in sales each year. Cruise lines put a great deal of emphasis on their food service. Industry surveys cite the food served shipboard as one of the top reasons for taking a cruise and selecting a specific line. Royal Caribbean International's 142,000-ton Voyager of the Seas carries 3,114 passengers and a crew of 1,181; fully 30 percent of the crew works in the kitchen. Royal Caribbean has won numerous international awards for its food.

Food service in airports and train terminals is often provided by restaurants—frequently limited-menu restaurants-and contract food companies such as ARAMARK that bid for the opportunity to sell food in the terminals.

United Airlines maintains its own in-flight kitchens; other airlines buy their meals from Ogden Entertainment Services (a division of ARAMARK), Sky Chef, or Dobbs International Services. Many airlines today are trying to differentiate themselves, at least on routes they share with several competing airlines, by serving more distinctive food in business and first-class sections, using fresh food instead of frozen items when possible. Even the selection of wines available on board has been greatly upgraded in some instances. Although airline passenger traffic is strong, growth in food and drink sales has reached a plateau, in part because food service on many flights has been cut back due to the growing popularity of no-frills air carriers such as Southwest and Midway.

Recreational market

The recreational market includes food service facilities located at sports arenas, stadiums, racetracks, movie theaters, bowling alleys, amusement parks, municipal convention centers, and other attractions. All together, this is an $11.7 billion market. In many cases, recreational-market food service facilities are concessions run by contract food companies. The largest contract food companies in the recreational market include Fine Host, Volume Services America, Ogden Entertainment Services, and ARAMARK.

Business and industry market

The business and industry market consists of nonfood service businesses that offer on-site food service to their employees. Most businesses that provide employee meals use contract food companies such as Sodexho and ARAMARK. At Pacific Bell in San Ramon, California, ARAMARK offers food service to 8,500 employees. A number of food stations serve such fare as Asian and Mexican dishes, sandwiches, salads, pizza, pasta, desserts, and specialty drinks called "smoothies."

Educational market

One of the biggest changes in college food service programmes has been the gradual shift from mandated meal plans to a la carte operations. Due in part to this shift, many college food service operators have become revenue producers instead of revenue consumers for their colleges.

Another change in college food service programmes has come about because an increasing number of nontraditional students are going to college today. Therefore, dining directors have had to change their food service programmes to accommodate preferences that are somewhat different from those of the typical 18-year-old.

Health care market

The health care market consists of three principal segments: hospitals and other medical centers, nursing homes, and retirement communities. Many experts believe that there is enormous potential for food service management companies in the health care market. This can be attributed to a combination of factorsrapidly changing life-styles, an aging population, skyrocketing medical costs, restricted federal funds, and a lack of family support systems.

Most health care facilities run their own food service departments, some of which can be quite extensive. Many hospitals operate vending machines, visitor coffee shops, employee cafeterias, special dining facilities for doctors, day-care food programmes for employees' children, regular patient food programmes, and special patient food programmes that can include gourmet meals (with accompanying wines) served in patient rooms.

Retail market

Two major trends in food service have surfaced in recent years. The first is the increasing tendency of Americans to eat food prepared outside of the home, as evidenced by the dramatic growth in restaurant food sales. The second trend, which is developing even more rapidly, is the growth in the take-out and delivery segment of the market. It is clear that Americans are cooking less. It is also clear that there is a growing inclination to buy food prepared outside the home and bring it home to consume it. This last development is in line with marketing trends in other areas such as home electronics and furniture, where research has shown that, at an increasing rate, people use their homes as recreational and entertainment centers.

A good part of retail business take-out sales comes at the expense of traditional restaurants and quick-service outlets. This is due, among other reasons, to increased marketing by convenience stores and supermarkets of their prepared take-out foods. Supermarkets are increasing the size and scope of their take-out food operations. Some industry observers expect the average supermarket to increase in size from its present 30,000-50,000 square feet to 200,000 square feet (2,790-4,650 square meters to 18,600 square meters). Much of that space will be devoted to precooked take-out dishes and sitdown food service areas.

Many supermarkets already offer take-out salad bars in addition to their traditional deli sections. Using ovens in their bakeries, many of today's supermarkets are preparing a complete line of food products for their small in-store restaurants and cafeterias. Supermarket research shows that supermarket produce is perceived to be fresher than that sold in most restaurants. Some supermarkets are taking advantage of this perception by selling a wide range of freshly prepared salad and vegetable dishes. Another supermarket food service trend is the growth of food courts. Supermarket chains are installing food courts (similar to those found in shopping malls) in hopes of winning back some of the food dollars they have lost to restaurants.

Corrections food service

Correctional institutions-state and federal prisons and local jailsconstitute another segment of the food service industry. Correctional institutions often have a hard time attracting and retaining food service staff because they cannot offer much professional career growth. However, the unique challenge they do offer can be attractive to some people. A prison must offer a cyclical menu that is not overlay repetitive and has the flexibility to meet special religious and medical dietary needs, while still offering a bit of creativity in both preparation and presentation. Theft is another problem encountered by prison food service systems.

Stringent controls must be used. Food costs are a further constraint on operations. Correctional institutions often have limited budgets for food service; economies of scale can thus make a substantial difference in the type and variety of food that can be offered to inmates. Because they enjoy economies of scale, contract food companies are now successfully competing in this area.

Military food service

Military food service is a very specialised area. Nevertheless, it deserves mention because of its diversity in terms of geography, type of facility, and size. Jobs in military food service range from space shuttle food preparation to aircraft carrier or nuclear submarine mess operations to Army, Navy, Air Force, Marine, and Coast Guard officers' club management at bases all over the world. Both civilian and military personnel are employed by many of these facilities.

Contractors

Contract food management companies are the major operators of noncommercial food service. Two of the largest are ARAMARK and Sodexho Contract food management companies are hired to operate restaurants and other food service outlets in convention centers, sports arenas, tourist attractions, colleges and schools, office buildings, manufacturing plant_, and health care facilities. Contractors meet the need of businesses and other clients who want to provide food service to patrons and! or employees, yet do not want to get involved in an activity (preparing and serving food) that is outside their expertise. Contract food management companies offer numerous careers in restaurant management. Many contractors recruit on college campuses.

As increasing numbers of consumers want to either dine out or take prepared food home, the number of food-service operations has skyrocketed from 155,000 about 25 years ago to nearly 800,000 today. But there's still room in the market for your food-service business.

Shifting demographics and changing lifestyles are driving the surge in food-service businesses. Busy consumers don't have the time or inclination to cook. They want the flavour of fresh bread without the hassle of baking. They want tasty, nutritious meals without dishes to wash. In fact, the rise in popularity of to-go operations underscores some clear trends in the food-service industry. More and more singles, working parents and elderly people are demanding greater convenience in buying their meals and are turning to operations that provide that convenience.

Though the future looks bright for the food-service industry overall, there are no guarantees in this business. Even the most successful operators will tell you this isn't a "get rich quick" industry. It's more like a "work hard and make a living" industry. A hard reality is that many restaurants fail during their first year in business, frequently due to a lack of planning. Does this mean your food-service business must be an extremely complex operation? Not at all-in fact, the more streamlined you can make it, the better your chances for success.

Robert O., owner of a casual seafood restaurant, observes, "The restaurant business is a simple business that people make complicated." His formula for success is quality food, good service and great people-an approach that's worked for him for nearly two decades.

Restaurant Management

A restaurant is an establishment that serves prepared food and beverages to be consumed on the premises. The term covers a multiplicity of venues and a diversity of styles of cuisine. Restaurants are sometimes a feature of a larger complex, typically a hotel, where the dining amenities are provided for the convenience of the residents and, of course, for the hotel to maximise their potential revenue. Such restaurants are often also open to non-residents.

The term *restaurant* (from the French *restaurer*, to restore) first appeared in the 16th century, meaning "a food which restores", and referred specifically to a rich, highly flavoured soup. According to the Guinness Book of Records, the Sobrino de Botin in Madrid, Spain is the oldest restaurant in existence today. It opened in 1725.

The modern sense of the word was born around 1765 when a Parisian soup-seller named Boulanger opened his establishment. The first restaurant in the form that became standard (customers sitting down with individual portions at individual tables, selecting food from menus, during fixed opening hours) was the *Grand Taverne de Londres*, founded in 1782 by a man named Beauvilliers. Whilst inns and taverns were known from antiquity, these were establishments aimed at travellers, and in general locals would rarely eat there.

The restaurant became established in France after the French Revolution broke up catering guilds and forced the aristocracy to flee, leaving a retinue of servants with the skills to cook excellent food; whilst at the same time numerous provincials arrived in Paris with no family to cook for them. Restaurants were the means by which these two could be brought together — and the French tradition of dining out was born. In this period the star chef Auguste Escoffier, often credited with founding classic French cuisine, flourished, becoming known as the "Cook of Kings and the King of Cooks."

Restaurants then spread rapidly across the world, with the first in the United States (*Jullien's Restarator*) opening in Boston in 1794. Most however continued on the standard approach (*Service à la française*) of providing a shared meal on the table to which customers would then help themselves, something which encouraged them to eat rather quickly. The modern formal style of dining, where customers are given a plate with the food already arranged on it, is known as *Service à la russe*, as it is said to have been introduced to France by the Russian Prince Kurakin in the 1810s, from where it spread rapidly to England and beyond.

Kinds of Restaurant

In France, a brasserie is a cafe doubling as a restaurant and serving single dishes and other meals in a relaxed setting. A bistro is a familiar name for a cafe serving moderately priced simple meals in an unpretentious setting, especially in Paris; bistros have become increasingly popular with tourists. Mainly in the UK and other countries influenced by British culture, the pub (short for public house) today serves a similar dual menu, offering beer and other alcohol along with basic food fare. Traditionally, pubs were primarily drinking establishments, whereas the modern pub business relies on food as well, to the point where so-called gastropubs are known for their high-quality "pub food".

A dining car (restaurant car) or diner (but not "diner car," except in uninformed parlance) is a railroad passenger car that serves meals on a train in the manner of a full-service, sit-down restaurant. It is distinct from other types of railroad food-service cars that do not duplicate the full-service restaurant experience, principally cars of various types in which one purchases food from a walk-up counter to be consumed either within the car or elsewhere in the train. While dining cars are less common today than they were in the past, they still play a significant role in passenger railroading, especially on medium- and long-distance trains.

In the U.S., fast-food restaurants and take-outs have become so widespread that the traditional standard type is now sometimes referred to as a sit-down restaurant (a retronym). A common feature of fast food restaurants is a lack of cutlery or crockery, the customer is expected to eat the food directly from the disposable container it was served in using their hands.

There are various types of fast-food restaurant:

— one collects food from a counter and pays, then sits down and starts eating (self-service restaurant); sub-varieties:

— one collects ready portions

— one serves oneself from containers

— one is served at the counter

— a special procedure is that one first pays at the cash desk, collects a ticket and then goes to the food counter, where one gets the food in exchange for the ticket

— one orders at the counter; after preparation the food is brought to one's table; paying may be on ordering or after eating.

"Family style", or sometimes called *table d'hôte* ("host's table") in France, are restaurants that have a fixed menu and fixed price, usually with dinners seated at a communal table such as on bench seats. More common in the 19th and early 20th century, they can still be found in rural communities, or as theme restaurants, or in vacation lodges. There is no menu to choose from, rather food is brought out in courses, usually with communal serving dishes, like at a family meal. Typical examples can include crab-houses, German-style beer halls, BBQ restaurants, hunting/fishing lodges. Some normal restaurants will mix elements of family style, such as a table salad or bread bowl that is included as part of the meal.

Restaurant guides list the best places to eat. One of the most famous of these, in Western Europe, is the Michelin series of guides which accord from 1 to 3 stars to restaurants they perceive to be of high culinary merit. Restaurants with stars in the Michelin guide are formal, expensive establishments; in general the more stars awarded, the higher the prices. In the United States, the Mobil Travel Guides and the AAA rate restaurants on a similar 1 to 5 star (Mobil) or Diamond (AAA) scale. Three, four, and five star/diamond ratings are roughly equivalent to the Michelin one, two, and three star ratings while one and two star ratings typically indicate more casual places to eat. In 2005, Michelin released a New York City guide, its first for the United States. The popular Zagat Survey compiles individuals' comments about restaurants but does not pass an "official" critical assessment.

The largest restaurant and menu guide is MenuPix.com. They offer over 15,000 restaurant menus in cities such as New York, Los Angeles, Boston, DC and San Francisco. Nearly all major American newspapers employ restaurant critics and publish online dining guides for the cities they serve. American newspaper restaurant critics typically visit dining establishments anonymously and return several times so as to sample the entire menu. Newspaper restaurant guides, therefore, tend to provide the most thorough coverage of various cities' dining options.

Economics of restaurants

In economics, restaurants are the end of the supply chain in the foodservice industry. There is usually much competition in most cities since barriers to entry are relatively low, which means that for most restaurants, it is hard to make a profit. In most First World industrialized countries, restaurants are heavily regulated to ensure the health and safety of the customers. The typical restaurant owner faces many obstacles to success, including raising initial capital, finding competent and skilled labour, maintaining consistent and excellent food quality, maintaining high standards of safety, and the constant hassle of minimising potential liability for any food poisoning or accidents that may occur.

The restaurant industry includes many 'different types of facilities and markets. Social and economic trends have emerged to shape the restaurant industry. The most profound trend is the working woman. With a larger income, women view restaurants not only as an affordable way to dine, but also as a convenience for themselves and their family. Restaurants provide an alternative to the added stress of arriving home from the office and dropping everything to cook the family's evening meal. The increase in household incomes has created a desire and convenience for people to spend time dining away from home or ordering takeout meals. The association cites households with a pretax income of $30,000 or more spends a larger amount of time dining out.

In short, the increase in working women has created a larger household income in which people can afford to eat away from home. The mere convenience of avoiding a night of cooking over the stove after a long day at the office is enticing to many women and their families. This trend is expected to remain long-term as people's lives continue on a fast-paced schedule. Whether it's driving a son or daughter to a school function or staying late at the office, sitting down at home for a meal with the entire family is hard to come by. From a promotional products perspective, understanding the driving forces behind the changes in the restaurant industry will enable eatery owners to properly target the audience they decide to pursue.

Food Service Operations

Food service outlets in lodging operations range from gourmet restaurants to coffee shops and even quick-service outlets. Lodging food service sales are tremendous.

— *Transportation Market*. Travellers eat at highway stops; on airplanes, ships, and trains; at airport terminals and train stations; and at other facilities in the transportation market-a market that enjoys about $3.7 billion in sales each year. Cruise lines put a great deal of emphasis on their food service. Industry surveys cite the food served shipboard as one of the top reasons for taking a cruise and selecting a specific line. Royal Caribbean International's 142,000-ton Voyager of the Seas carries 3,114 passengers and a crew of 1,181; fully 30 percent of the crew works in the kitchen. Royal Caribbean has won numerous international awards for its food. Food service in airports and train terminals is often provided by restaurants—frequently limited-menu restaurants-and contract food companies such as ARAMARK that bid for the opportunity to sell food in the terminals.

Many airlines today are trying to differentiate themselves, at least on routes they share with several competing airlines, by serving more distinctive food in business and first-class sections, using fresh food instead of frozen items when possible. Even the selection of wines available on board has been greatly upgraded in some instances. Although airline passenger traffic is strong, growth in food and drink sales has reached a plateau, in part because food service on many flights has been cut back due to the growing popularity of no-frills air carriers such as Southwest and Midway.

— *Recreational Market*. The recreational market includes food service facilities located at sports arenas, stadiums, racetracks, movie theaters, bowling alleys, amusement parks, municipal convention centers, and other attractions. All together, this is an $11.7 billion market. In many cases, recreational-market food service facilities are concessions run by contract food companies.

— *Business and Industry Market*. The business and industry market consists of nonfood service businesses that offer on-site food service to their employees. Most businesses that provide employee meals use contract food companies such as Sodexho and ARAMARK. At Pacific Bell in San Ramon, California, ARAMARK offers food service to 8,500 employees. A number of food stations serve such fare as Asian and Mexican dishes, sandwiches, salads, pizza, pasta, desserts, and specialty drinks called "smoothies."

— *Educational Market*. One of the biggest changes in college food service programmes has been the gradual shift from mandated meal plans to a la carte operations. Due in part to this shift, many college food service operators have become revenue producers instead of revenue consumers for their colleges. Another change in college food service programmes has come about because an increasing number of nontraditional students are going to college today. Therefore, dining directors have had to change their food service programmes to accommodate preferences that are somewhat different from those of the typical 18-year-old.

— *Health Care Market*. The health care market consists of three principal segments: hospitals and other medical centers, nursing homes, and retirement communities (including congregate food sites-community-sponsored meal centers for senior citizens). Many experts believe that there is enormous potential for food service management companies in the health care market. This can be attributed to a combination of factorsra- pidly changing life-styles, an aging population, skyrocketing medical costs, restricted federal funds, and a lack of family support systems. Most health care facilities run their own food service departments, some of which can be quite extensive. Many hospitals operate vending machines, visitor coffee shops, employee cafeterias, special dining facilities for doctors, day-care food programmes for employees' children, regular patient food programmes, and special patient food programmes that can include gourmet meals (with accompanying wines) served in patient rooms.

— *Retail Market*. Two major trends in food service have surfaced in recent years. The first is the increasing tendency of Americans to eat food prepared outside of the home, as evidenced by the dramatic growth in restaurant food sales. The second trend, which is developing even more rapidly, is the growth in the take-out and delivery segment of the market. It is clear that Americans are cooking less. It is also clear that there is a growing inclination to buy food prepared outside the home and bring it home to consume it. This last development is in line with marketing trends in other areas such as home electronics and furniture, where research has shown that, at an increasing rate, people use their homes as recreational and entertainment centers.

Some industry observers expect the average supermarket to increase in size from its present 30,000-50,000 square feet to 200,000 square feet (2,790-4,650 square meters to 18,600 square meters). Much of that space will be devoted to precooked take-out dishes and sitdown food service areas. Many supermarkets already offer take-out salad bars in addition to their traditional deli sections. Using ovens in their bakeries, many of today's supermarkets are preparing a complete line of food products for their small in-store restaurants and cafeterias.

Supermarket research shows that supermarket produce is perceived to be fresher than that sold in most restaurants. Some supermarkets are taking advantage of this perception by selling a wide range of freshly prepared salad and vegetable dishes. Some have hired chefs to work in open kitchens so that customers can actually see that dishes are prepared with fresh-not frozen-ingredients. Another supermarket food service trend is the growth of food courts. Supermarket chains are installing food courts (similar to those found in shopping malls) in hopes of winning back some of the food dollars they have lost to restaurants.

Correctional institutions often have a hard time attracting and retaining food service staff because they cannot offer much professional career growth. However, the unique challenge they do offer can be attractive to some people. A prison must offer a cyclical menu that is not overlay repetitive and has the flexibility to meet special religious and medical dietary needs, while still offering a bit of creativity in both preparation and presentation. Theft is another problem encountered by prison food service systems. Stringent controls must be used. Food costs are a further constraint on operations. Correctional institutions often have limited budgets for food service; economies of scale can thus make a substantial difference in the type and variety of food that can be offered to inmates.

Contract food management companies offer numerous careers in restaurant management. Many contractors recruit on college campuses. As increasing numbers of consumers want to either dine out or take prepared food home, the number of food-service operations has skyrocketed from 155,000 about 25 years ago to nearly 800,000 today. But there's still room in the market for your food-service business. Shifting demographics and changing lifestyles are driving the surge in food-service businesses. Busy consumers don't have the time or inclination to cook. They want the flavour of fresh bread without the hassle of baking. They want tasty, nutritious meals without dishes to wash.

In fact, the rise in popularity of to-go operations underscores some clear trends in the food-service industry. More and more singles, working parents and elderly people are demanding greater convenience in buying their meals and are turning to operations that provide that convenience. Though the future looks bright for the food-service industry overall, there are no guarantees in this business. Even the most successful operators will tell you this isn't a "get rich quick" industry. It's more like a "work hard and make a living" industry. A hard reality is that many restaurants fail during their first year in business, frequently due to a lack of planning.

5

Clubs, Gaming and Casino Industry

The club industry is still evolving, conforming to today's social trends and population demands. There are more than 11,000 private clubs today. Of those, nearly 8,500 are "total facility" clubs which specialise in food and beverage, exercise, golf, tennis, boating, squash, racquetball and other activities.

Clubs have been around for hundreds of years, but most clubs in existence today are patterned after those of the British from the seventeenth and eighteenth centuries. The Royal and Ancient Golf Club of St. Andrews, Scotland, founded in 1758 and said to be the birthplace of golf, is the forerunner of the modern country club. Today's city clubs are similarly related to English social clubs, where members meet over drinks and dinner in local taverns. For example, the Mermaid Club, founded by Sir Walter Raleigh and attended by Marlowe and Shakespeare, met at London's Mermaid Tavern.

Club ownership can be categorised into two major types: equity and proprietary. The equity club, historically the oldest type and still the most common ownership structure, is a not-forprofit club. It is typically owned and organised by its members for their own enjoyment. A board of directors, elected by the membership, regulates the budget and establishes the club's policy. The club's general manager is hired by and reports to the board of directors. Excess money from club operations and dues is reinvested in improvements to the club's services or facilities.

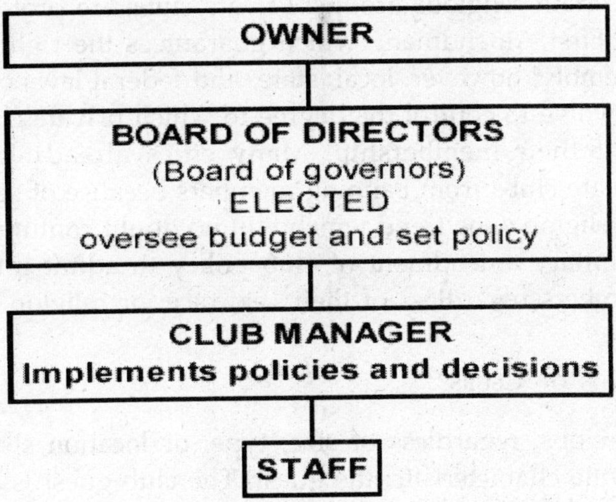

Figure 1. Organisation chart of equity clubs

The Corporate / Developer or Proprietary club is owned by an individual or company, and operates for profit. Individuals purchase a membership from the club's owner or owners. Proprietary clubs allow members limited input and control of the club's management decisions. The general manager reports to the club owner.

Clubs have always restricted their membership, whether to alumni of a particular school, residents of a particular community, members of a particular profession, or believers in a shared religious faith. In fact, membership in some clubs can only be obtained upon the invitation and recommendation of one or more current members. Private clubs, by their very nature, are selective.

Clubs have often been accused of deliberately discriminating against women, minorities, and members of certain religious groups. Private clubs are protected by the First Amendment, which guarantees the right of free assembly; however, local, state, and federal laws continue to evolve to control the degree to which private clubs can limit their membership. Many cities already prohibit private clubs from banning members because of sex, race, or religion. One trend which will no doubt continue is the voluntary amendment of club policy to admit interested members regardless of their sex, race, or religion.

Kinds of Clubs

All clubs, regardless of size, type, or location share one unique characteristic: the guest. The club guest is a dues-paying member, one who has a financial and possibly an emotional connection to the club. Many club charge both an initiation fee and an annual membership fee. The initiation fee for an exclusive country club may run as high as $150,000, although most clubs charge far less. An interesting statistic about clubs in America is that 80 percent of clubs are golf and country clubs; approximately nine percent are city clubs.

Private Clubs

Most private clubs are country clubs that provide recreational and social facilities, usually in a suburban setting. The primary recreational activities of the country club is golf, but swimming and tennis are also standard pursuits. In addition, some country clubs may offer horseback riding, billiard rooms, aerobic facilities, sauna or steam baths, and other activities for their members' enjoyment. Most country clubs operate at least one dining room, along with extensive dining and banquet facilities. Members commonly hold weddings, reunions, or other social events there.

In recent years some country clubs have been built as part of an upscale community development project. The presence of a neighbourhood country club may attract a significant number of new-home buyers to a region. Clubhouse amenities often include the club's pro shop, locker rooms, fitness centers and dining facilities. It is common for a club to offer a variety of food and beverage outlets including formal and casual dining, snack bars and banquet facilities.

The general manager of a country club generally has a large and broad range of roles and responsibilities. These responsibilities may include, but are not limited to, overseeing the development and construction of new tennis courts, a new golf course and a major clubhouse renovation; managing land and other property; overseeing the repair and maintenance of all athletic facilities; purchasing equipment; overseeing the food and beverage operation; overall responsibility of the club's financial management; and acting as a liaison between the club's board of directors, staff and membership. Country clubs sell both full and partial memberships. The social membership, for example, may enable the member to use the dining room, meeting rooms, and pool, but not the golf or tennis facilities.

City Clubs

These facilities, usually housed in a building or part of a building located within a city or a suburban office complex, range from luncheon-only clubs that serve segments of the business community to fully integrated dining and athletic clubs. As in most clubs, the goal is to provide a place for individuals with similar interests to dine and socialise together.

Various amenities a city club may offer its members include, but are not limited to, multiple food and beverage outlets, both casual and formal; meeting rooms; indoor sports facilities (billiard rooms, swimming pools); libraries; and overnight accommodations. City clubs promote trade, business, and friendship among colleagues. As the name implies, city clubs are found in cities or business districts.

A tremendous variation exists among city clubs, in terms of facilities size and purpose, but most offer top-quality food service to members and their guests. City clubs may be organised around a certain profession, such as the Press club in Washington, D.C., and the Lawyers' Club in New York City. They may be associated with a particular college or university and restrict membership to alumni, faculty, and staff of the university. Most city clubs do not restrict membership to such a narrowly defined group, but may attract business-leaders and professionals from a variety of fields.

Kinds of city clubs

— Athletic

— Dining

— Professional

— Social

— University

Other Clubs

Military clubs: The U.S. Department of Defence provides clubs for its officers and noncommissioned officers. Located near some of its major military institutions, these clubs have dining and meeting-room facilities; some also have beaches, recreational facilities, and lodging accommodations.

Yacht clubs: Yacht clubs are designed to promote and regulate boating and yachting. Typically, the yacht club owns and operates a marina for its members. The club may also run a clubhouse with dining and recreation facilities.

Faternal clubs: Although less prestigious than many city and country clubs, fraternal clubs such as the Shriners, Elks, and Veterans of Foreign Wars (VFW) enjoy large memberships in some parts of the country. Usually such clubs own a facility available to members for banquets, weddings, and other special events. Food services may be operated by the fraternal club as well.

Nature of Clubs

The unique nature of clubs and their membership status raises the service requirements and expectations of guests. Clubs, by their very nature and definition are selective. Members want to feel like the service they receive is different, a step above that available to others. This raises the demands on all those who work for clubs, but especially for the general manager, who must meet a host of sometimes divergent goals. The first priority of a club manager is member satisfaction. A club manager must be diplomatic, provide exemplary service, prepare the budget, and oversee the entire operation. Most club managers are not recent graduates; instead, they often come from the ranks of hotel management and are at a later stage in their careers.

The job of assistant manager is usually an entry-level position for a college graduate with a degree in hospitality management. An assistant manager might be in charge of food and beverage operations, supervising the purchase and service of food and beverages in the dining room and lounges. In this case the assistant manager would work closely with the chef, who is in charge of the kitchen, or the purchaser, who is in charge of the expenditure of club funds.

Other areas of responsibility for the assistant manager include the athletic facilities, as well as the security and maintenance of the club-house itself. A large club might have more than one assistant manager to oversee specific areas of the club.

For those interested in club management, the Club Managers Association of America (CMAA) serves as the professional association for club managers. Founded in 1927, CMAA offers educational opportunities for its members, publishes the trade journal Club Management, and provides a certification programme for participants. This programme includes a comprehensive examination in addition to coursework that enables a successful participant to attain the title "Certified Club Manager." For those who enjoy the challenge of providing the best, the club career may be of interest.

Club Income

— Annual gross revenue is more than $11.33 billion for all clubs.

— Food and beverage revenues equal $3.79 billion.

— The average club income is $4.9 million.

Club Employees

— Clubs employ more than 302,830 people.
— Club payrolls equal $4.4 billion.

Club Outreach Programmes

— Clubs annually raise close to $165 million for charity.
— Clubs recently gave a total of $8.3 million in student scholarships.
— Most of CMAA's 50 chapters sponsor scholarship funds.

Economic Impact of Clubs

— The average clubs spends $1.6 million in the local community.
— A typical club pays $132,449 in property taxes.
— The average club spends $1.9 million within the state as a whole.
— Overall, club operations generate $3.07 billion for state economies around the country.

Club membership has increased steadily over the last 20 years and will continue to do so. Due to this growth, the concept of the club has changed remarkably. Throughout the history of clubs, dramatic changes in the services and amenities offered to members. As managers, the future no longer lies solely in country clubs. There is now a wider scope of clubs including athletic, city, military, swimming, tennis, university, riding and yacht clubs with additional opportunities for advancement.

To provide a better understanding of the services provided and the manager's role in a particular type of club, a description of the two most common types of clubs country. In addition to controlling daily operations, a manager may be required to have a familiarity with antiques and the scholarly arts and should possess knowledge of wine. Because of the club's character and location, a city club manager can generally expect the heaviest use of club facilities in the afternoon hours during the business week.

Countless jobs exist in the club industry and are described in the Job Descriptions for the Private Club Industry published by Club Managers Association of America. Club managers' duties vary based on experience, size and location of the club and also the number of employees that one supervises. For example, in a small club that employs fewer than 20 people, the manager must be a "jack-of-all-trades," heading various departments and supervising employees. At a larger club operation with hundreds or even thousands of members, the club manager may act as a supervisory head, who is the main contact for the department heads and the liaison between the board members and the staff.

The following are just some of the available job opportunities in clubs:

— General Manager

— Chief Executive Officer

— Operating Officer

— Clubhouse Manager

— Assistant Manager

— Golf Course Superintendent

— Food and Beverage Director

— Pro Shop Manager

— Executive Housekeeper

— Dining Room Manager

— Chef

— Catering Manager

— Controller

As in most professions, formal education and practical experience are necessary in attaining a management-level position. Students are encouraged to participate in internships, externships and co-ops in order to gain the experience that managers are looking for in prospective, full-time employees.

Based on experience, one may be offered an assistant or mid-management position upon graduation, which may lead to a management position with increased responsibility. You may find that many of today's successful club managers began their professional careers in fields other than a formal hospitality or business training programme. However, in recent years, a trend in managers possessing degrees in business and hospitality with a concentration directly relating to the club industry. The completion of your education, in combination with internships and work experience in the industry, will improve your chances for professional success.

Club Manager Qualification

While basic managerial skills are required at every club, specific requirements will vary with each individual. In order to be a successful club manager, one must be familiar with all aspects of club operations, including:

— Accounting and Finance

— Building and Facilities Management

— Food and Beverage

— Recreation Management

— External and Government Influences Management

— Technology

— Management and Marketing

— Club Governance

— Human and Professional Resources

Salary and Benefits

Earning potential for the club manager is excellent. Although salaries vary with club type and geographical location, assistant managers on average earn $49,000 per year, based on the individual's experience and education. The average salary for clubhouse managers is $54,400 and the average salary for general managers is $96,500 per year. The average salary for those holding the title of Chief Operating Officer is $121,000. In addition, many clubs offer bonuses, housing, health and retirement packages, as well as vacation and clothing allowances. This may bring the total compensation package to well over $152,700 for a seasoned professional.

Related Jobs

The job of a club manager is comparable to that of a hotel or restaurant manager in that each position requires a competence in administrative and operational procedures, public relations and financial management. The manager of a club benefits from a more personal relationship with his or her members. As a group, club members are less transient than the guests of a hotel or restaurant. This allows club managers a greater chance to develop their talents and form a stronger bond with their members.

Role of General Manager (GM)

Serves as Chief Operating Officer of the club: manages all aspects of the club including its activities and the relationships between the club and its Board of Directors, members, guests, employees, community, government and industry. Coordinates and administers the club's policies as defined by its Board of Directors. Develops operating policies and procedures and directs the work of all department managers. Implements and monitors the budget, monitors the quality of the club's products and services and ensures maximum member and guest satisfaction. Secures and protects the club's assets, including facilities and equipment.

Duties of general manager

— Implements general policies established by the Board of Directors; directs their administration and execution.

— Plans, develops and approves specific operational policies, programmes, procedures and methods in concert with general policies.

— Coordinates the development of the club's long range and annual (business) plans

— Develops, maintains and administers a sound organisational plan; initiates improvements as necessary.

— Establishes a basic personnel policy; initiates and monitors policies relating to personnel actions and training and professional development programmes.

— Maintains membership with the Club Managers Association of America and other professional associations. Attends conferences, workshops and meetings to keep abreast of current information and developments in the field.

— Coordinates development of operating and capital budgets according to the budget calendar; monitors monthly and other financial statements for the club; takes effective corrective action as required.

— Coordinates and serves as ex-officio member of appropriate club committees.

— Welcomes new club members; "meets and greets" all club members as practical during their visits to the club.

— Provides advice and recommendations to the President and committees about construction, alterations, maintenance, materials, supplies, equipment and services not provided in approved plans and/or budgets.

— Consistently assures that the club is operated in accordance with all applicable local, state and federal laws.

— Oversees the care and maintenance of all the club's physical assets and facilities.

— Coordinates the marketing and membership relations programmes to promote the club's services and facilities to potential and present members.

— Ensures the highest standards for food, beverage, sports and recreation, entertainment and other club services.

— Establishes and monitors compliance with purchasing policies and procedures.

— Reviews and initiates programmes to provide members with a variety of popular events.

— Analyses financial statements, manages cash flow and establishes controls to safeguard funds. Reviews income and costs relative to goals; takes corrective action as necessary.

— Works with subordinate department heads to schedule, supervise and direct the work of all employees.

— Attends meetings of the club's Executive Committee and Board of Directors.

— Participates in outside activities that are judged as appropriate and approved by the Board of Directors to enhance the prestige of the club; broadens the scope of the club's operation by fulfilling the public obligations of the club as a participating member of the community.

Gaming and Casino Hotels

While some may think that gambling is a recent phenomenon, it actually dates back to antiquity. Dice have been recovered from Egyptian tombs, while the Chinese, Japanese, Greeks and Romans all were known to play games of skill and chance for amusement as early as 2300 B.C. Both Native Americans and European colonists brought a history of gambling from their own cultures that helped shape America's views and practices. Native Americans developed games and language describing gambling and believed that their gods determined fate and chance. In 1643, explorer Roger Williams wrote about the games of chance developed by the Narragansett Indians of Rhode Island.

British colonisation of America was partly financed through lottery proceeds, beginning in the early 17th century. Because lotteries were viewed as a popular form of voluntary taxation in England during the Georgian era, they also became popular in America as European settlers arrived here. Half-dozen lotteries sponsored by prominent individuals such as Ben Franklin, John Hancock and George Washington operated in each of the 13 colonies to raise funds for building projects. Between 1765 and 1806, Massachusetts authorised lotteries to help build dormitories and supply equipment for Harvard

College; many other institutions of higher learning, including Dartmouth, Yale and Columbia, also were financed through lotteries. A lottery even was approved to finance the American Revolution.

Tribal Gaming

Gaming has been a part of the United States from the colonial era up through today. Lotteries were critical to funding the Revolutionary War, and the colonisation of America, and even helped fund the beginning of venerable institutions like Harvard University and Princeton.

Indian gaming, originally part of tribal ceremonies or celebrations, existed long before Europeans came to America. However, as Europeans began settling America, they gradually took away every means of self-sufficiency American Indians had: destroying agrarian societies, killing the buffalo and forcing American Indians onto remote, desolate reservations. Today, gaming is often the only viable source of employment and governmental revenues available to tribes.

Today, gaming has replaced the buffalo as the mechanism used by American Indian people for survival. The proceeds from gaming are used by Indian Nations for subsistence, cultural preservation, and to replenish impoverished economies. Indian gaming has been a major catalyst for community growth and economic development, generating revenues for tribes like no federal stimulus effort ever has before. After decades of poverty and high unemployment on often geographically remote reservations, Indian people now see gaming as an integral part of tribal economies and the means to achieve self-sufficiency. But maintaining the sovereign right to conduct tribal gaming operations hasn't gone unchallenged, and opposition from state and federal governments and privately held gaming interests still grows.

In 1988, Congress formally recognised but limited the right of Indians to conduct gaming operations with the passage of the Indian Gaming Regulatory Act (IGRA). States lobbied vigorously for IGRA and for the compacting provisions over tribal objections. The IGRA requires tribes to negotiate with states concerning games to be played and regulation while it ensures that tribal governments are the sole owners and primary beneficiaries of gaming, and legislatively recognises tribal gaming as a way of promoting economic development for tribes.

Early casinos in Europe

Before the establishment of casinos, gambling games were conducted on the streets, in homes, or in private clubs. (The word "casino" comes from the Italian "casa", which means house.) The amount that could be won was limited to the funds of the individual players. By the 17th century however, gambling had become formalised, with special venues that offered players the opportunity to bet against the "house", which would act as banker, paying out all winnings and retaining losing bets. This gave players the advantage of potentially winning more money than they bet.

Edouard Benazet, who employed Parisian craftsmen to design the stylish rooms, opened one of the oldest casinos in Europe, at Baden Baden in Germany, in 1748. Despite several closures in its history, the Baden Baden casino still operates today.

The casino at Spa, a Belgian resort town noted for its mineral baths, was built by the Prince Bishop of the province of Liege in 1763. In 1857, Prince Charles III of Monaco decided to introduce gambling to his Mediterranean principality to boost its finances. Under the auspices of art lover Francoise Blanc and his son Camille, no expense was spared on the "belle epoque building" which was created by a number of architects, among them Charles Garnier, designer of the Paris Opera House. In the early 20th century Monte Carlo Casino quickly became a fashionable destination for the rich and famous of the day, including the director of the "Ballet Russe" in Paris, Sergei Diaghalev, Britain's King Edward VII, and the Italian tenor Enrico Caruso.

Gaming in the USA

Some of the first casinos in American were established during the early 1800s in New Orleans, along the Mississippi River. Although, at that time, there were no casinos on the riverboats themselves, informal gambling was a popular way for travellers to pass the journey. Professional gamblers, called "sharps", would target wealthy passengers and relieve them of their money. Gambling moved westward with the expansion of the railroads and flourished during the time of the California gold rush and the Nevada silver era.

Las Vegas in Nevada owes its success to the mobster Benjamin "Bugsy" Siegel who organised gaming and bookmaking operations for The Mob (the Mafia). Due to a crackdown on gambling in the eastern USA, Siegel moved west in the 1940s. During the Great Depression gambling had been legalised in Nevada to increase revenue for the state, but what existed in Las Vegas at that time were a few decidedly down-market casinos that were frequented by the locals.

Siegel planned to open a luxurious hotel where the rich and famous could gamble and, after a failed attempt to take over an existing casino, he decided to build his own. Once Siegel had managed to convince The Mob to invest in his idea, building started, but costs escalated from initial estimates of $1.2 million to over $6 million, because everyone, including Siegel, was stealing money from the project. It is rumoured that the palm trees were sold to the casino several times over and that Siegel's girlfriend, Virginia Hill, was accumulation money in a Swiss bank account. The Mob soon discovered Siegel's skimming and ordered him to be killed, but decided to give him a reprieve until after the opening.

The Flamingo Hotel and Casino finally opened on 26 December 1946. A huge party was organised, with many of the film stars of the day in attendance. The hotel was not finished, so the guests had nowhere to sleep. They parties for two days and then went home. The Flamingo was a flop and Bugsy Siegel was eventually killed by The Mob in 1947, but his dream of making Las Vegas into a gambling canter survived.

As other businessmen realised that Las Vegas had potential as a resort, investment flowed into the town. The Desert Inn Casino opened in 1950, followed by the Sands Casino in 1952, with the Dunes, and the Riviera opening in 1955. Despite gambling being illegal, casinos continued to operate elsewhere in the USA thanks to widespread corruption in the police and government. One of the most luxurious "illegal" casinos was Chicago's Big House which operated between 1929 and 1950. Run by associates of gangster Al Capone, it was elegantly furnished, with mahogany gaming tables, oriental rugs and a free taxi service to shuttle players to and from Chicago's southside. The club was also the headquarters of a countrywide bookmaking operation.

During the 1950s virtually all the casinos in Las Vegas were controlled by The Mob. A US senate investigation into criminal activity in the casino industry found that skimming (retaining a portion of the profits) was rife, resulting in tax evasion on stakes and profits. When legislation allowing corporations to own Las Vegas casinos came into being in 1965, entrepreneur and multi-millionaire Howard Hughes was the first to take advantage of this change in law, buying the Desert Inn and several other casinos, as well as plots of land in the city. When MGM, Hilton and Holiday Inn followed suit, the finances of the mob proved to be no match for the might of the major corporations, and gradually the casino industry was cleaned up.

Sports betting

A feature of many casinos are the sports books (facilities where betting takes place on horse races and other sporting events). Frank Rosenthal, a US horse racing handicapper who realised that bookmaking could be a huge money-spinner for casinos, opened the first race and sports book at the Stardust Casinos in Las Vegas. Its success resulted in race and sports books being introduced to The Strip. The story of Rosenthal's life was portrayed in the movie "Casino".

Today's gaming

Studies have shown that today's casino players are typically graduates in white-collar jobs with a higher than average income, who gamble to win money. A survey carried out by Roper Starch Worldwide Inc. of New York found that, for three out of four casino visitors, their prime motive is to win, while 57 per cent go for entertainment and recreation. Australians are the western world's biggest gamblers, spending over $2,000 a year per head of population. A close second are Americans at $1,800 per head of population.

Casinos operate around the world, mainly in tourist areas including Las Vegas, Australia's Gold Coast, and resorts in the Mediterranean and Caribbean. Gaming is mostly state controlled and is an important contributor to national and local revenues, although percentages vary from country to country. Gaming is a huge industry in the USA, where it is legal in 24 states. There has been a casino building boom in recent years, particularly in Nevada. Gambling was legalised in Atlantic City, New Jersey, in 1978, to revitalise the rundown seaside resort.

In 1987, after a legal battle, the US Supreme Court finally recognised the right of native Americans to operate gaming establishments on their reservations. Since 1989, over 300 new gaming operations have been established on Indian reservations. The largest casino in the world, Foxwoods Resort in Connecticut, is owned and operated by the Mashantucket Tribe and attracts over 16 million visitors annually. It comprises two hotels and five separate casinos. Foxwoods has 140,000m2 (1,5 million sq ft) of floor space, of which 28,000m2 (300,000 sq ft) is devoted to gaming.

Las Vegas reigns supreme as the "casino capital" of the world, attracting 30 million visitors annually to over 50 casinos. When Wilbur Clark opened the Desert Inn on 24 April 1950, he ceremonially threw away the keys, announcing there would never be a reason to lock the door again. The tradition continues today, with most Las

Vegas casinos opening 24 hours, seven days a week. The minimum age for gambling in Nevada is 21 years.

The 1960s saw the legalisation in the UK. Bringing the gaming industry within the law led to the implementation of strict controls to regulate payouts and how the games operate. The Gaming Board of Great Britain ensures the fair running of casinos and scrutinizes casino personnel and operators. Of the UK's 116 casinos, 21 are located in London, with the remainder in major cities and tourist areas. Almost all countries in continental Europe have casinos. France has government regulated casinos in over 170 towns and cities. Spain legalised casinos in the late 1970s and also allows slot machines in bars and arcades.

In the Netherlands, a government company, Holland Casinos, was established to operate the casinos, which now exist in ten locations. Greece has nine casinos, which are privately-run government-allocated franchises. Belgium's eight casinos remain illegal but are tolerated by the government, which imposes taxation on them. In the 1970s casinos were legalised in Australia. They are run by private operators under franchises granted by the government. Fourteen casinos now operate in the major cities and Gold Coast resorts, contributing a $2 billion annually to state revenues.

Canada began opening government-owned casinos in the early 1990s and now has a number of resort casinos that attract tourists, as well as some smaller provincial casinos catering for the local population. Although South Africa introduced casino gaming during the apartheid era, confining it to the so-called "independent homelands", the demise of apartheid meant that the country had to face up to the reality of legalising gaming operations that were formerly not considered to be within the boundaries of the state. Casino gaming was recognised in 1994 and a rationalisation process, under the Gambling Board, has ensured that lucrative gaming licenses are equitable distributed throughout all nine provinces.

In many countries, gambling has gone in and out of favour depending on the prevailing moral, social and religious climate. Most objections to gambling are based on social and religious issues. However despite numerous attempts throughout history to outlaw gaming, it has still thrived. Banning gaming simply results in the establishments of illegal casinos.

Gaming-related social problems are as old as gaming itself. In Roman times, gaming was restricted to one week of the year, during the Saturnalia festival (equivalent to the Christmas and New Year holidays). However this did not deter Roman players, who continued to gamble in private houses and clubs. Even when fines (equivalent to four times the stakes) were introduced for players caught gambling, the Romans managed to evade the law by using engraved discs, called "roundels", instead of money.

Almost as soon as playing cards were introduced to Europe, they were opposed. In Paris, legislation prohibiting playing cards was passed in 1377, and in Italy, playing cards and dice were burned. In the USA, many attempts were made to prevent gambling. Early Puritan settlers initially banned the possession of gaming equipment, but relented, allowing games for recreational purposes. Later legislation was ineffective as it banned specific games. Players simply changed the names or invented new games. By 1910 gambling was made illegal throughout the USA, but due to widespread corruption among law enforcement officers, this law had little effect.

In the 54 years since the first legal wager was made in sparsely populated Las Vegas in 1931, the gaming industry has evolved into one of the most dynamic and economically powerful forces in present-day American business. With some form of gaming now legal in 48 of the 50 states and the now-dominant view that gaming is an enjoyable and morally acceptable form of entertainment, the gaming business is currently a $500 billion venture responsible for hundreds of thousands of jobs and billions of dollars in tax revenues and capital investment. It provides a strong economic impact that has repeatedly proven to be a financial boost for governments and the citizens these governments serve.

Buoyed by the success of gaming in Nevada and the tax-free status Nevada residents enjoy, gaming first expanded to Atlantic City in 1978. Before casino gaming was introduced in Atlantic City, the area had all but been abandoned by tourists, leading to a decay in both its social and physical stature. While casinos in Atlantic City have been criticized for failing short of completely revitalising the area, the simple fact remains that without casinos Atlantic City would not have 41,000 gaming industry jobs, would not have an annual direct tax impact of $600 million, would not have $5 billion in new capital investment related to gaming and would not have 10 times more annual tourist visits than in the years preceding gaming's introduction.

As day-to-day costs began to outstrip tax revenues during the early-to-mid-1 980s and as unemployment rates soared and retail sales dropped, state and local governments began seeking other forms of revenue and economic development. This created the birth of the riverboat gaming industry—and the 'face of the entertainment business in the United States would forever be changed. Beginning with Iowa in 1989 and continuing with Mississippi, Illinois, Louisiana, Missouri and Indiana, states heeded the voters' wishes and began legalising riverboat gaming, which in turn brought a new form of entertainment to millions of people far away from the major gaming centers of Nevada and Atlantic City. Land-based casinos in Colorado and South Dakota and Native American gaming ventures in many other states also contributed to the growing availability of what had been perceived as taboo decades earlier.

If you combined all of the commercial gaming activities in the country and created one entity, it would account for $39.9 billion in revenue in 1994, a figure that would rank 12th among all companies on the Forbes Sales 500 list based on gross revenue being equivalent to sales in non-gambling accounting. This figure, for example, ranks ahead of Kmart's $34.3 billion but below Chrysler's $52.2 billion. In terms of aggregate sales, the Forbes Sales 500 increased by a healthy 8 percent in 1994, but gaming did even better, increasing 15 percent over the previous year.

So what do all these numbers prove? In simple terms, they show what a force gaming has become in relation to the national economy as a whole. With more than 90 gaming companies traded publicly, the national impact of gaming is felt on Wall Street and in small towns throughout the country. The numbers also indicate this country's growing demand for entertainment, an appetite that is directly related to a 6 percent rise in personal income from 1993 to 1994. Proportionally, more and more discretionary income is spent on various forms of entertainment, which includes sporting events, concerts, theme parks, movies and, of course, gaming.

Gaming is certainly not a cure-all for every state facing a budget shortfall, but under the right circumstances, gaming can produce remarkable economic benefits that create long-term stability and improve the overall quality of life. For examples on how to implement casino gaming to produce an undisputed level of success, look no further than Vicksburg, Mississippi, Joliet, Illinois, and Council Bluffs, Iowa.

Prior to the legalisation of gaming, Vicksburg, population 30,000, was "in a very tough situation," local clothing store owner John Wayne Jabour said. "We really shrunk in the last 10 years. From 1980 to 1990 we lost almost 15,000 people in our community and things were just headed downward. Stores were closing right and left, you couldn't sell a piece of property, you couldn't sell a home..."

And now?

"People have a spring in their walk, they're happy, they're optimistic," Jabour said. Jabour is certainly not alone in his assessment of gaming's positive effects in the Vicksburg area. "Well, Vicksburg had been essentially stagnant until gaming came to town," Pete Stone of the Vicksburg Warren Chamber of Commerce said. "You can only do so much with the Chamber. We've gone through the same recruiting process and so forth and so on, but the advent of gaming coming here has helped us a great deal economically, obviously, and it's virtually wiped out unemployment."

"Gaming has been a real boost to Vicksburg's tourism industry," Executive Director of the Vicksburg Convention and Visitors Bureau Lenore Barkley said. "We were a tourism destination before gaming, but this has been a real asset in that it gives our visitors one more reason to come to Vicksburg and has our visitors maybe staying longer." According to figures from the Mississippi Department of Economic and Community Development, tourism-related spending in Vicksburg—money not spent at the city's four casinos—jumped $10 million to $78.5 million the first year casinos were open.

The Vicksburg Convention and Visitors Bureau derives operating income from a 1 -cent sales tax collected only on nightly room rentals and tabs at larger-volume restaurants. This tax generated $415,000 in 1992, the first year casinos opened, $459,000 in 1993 and $636,000 in 1994. The influx of tourists has also contributed to a rise in nonresident retail sales, which climbed from $25.4 million in 1993 to $26.6 million in 1994. "Tourism's always been very important to the stability of this community and now with gaming there's noboy in this city that isn't touched by the extra revenue that's being brought into the city," Barkley said.

"We are living in good times now. It is absolutely amazing what gaming has done for this area," Vicksburg Warren Chamber of Commerce Executive Vice President Jimmy Ware told the Vicksburg Evening Post. In Joliet, population 88,000, the turnaround has been just as remarkable. Perhaps an October 1995 special report in The Baltimore Sun summed up the impact of gaming the best:

"Five years ago, this was a typical rust belt city of shuttered stores, crumbling sidewalks and empty streets. Today, thousands of tourists step along red brick walkways lined with honey locust trees. The city's change in fortune is largely the result of four riverboat casinos docked along the banks of the Des Plaines River. Since opening in 1992, the hulking ships have brought nearly 4,000 jobs and $67 million in tax revenue to Joliet. More significantly, perhaps, they have enhanced the economy without increasing crime or hurting local businesses, according to police data and interviews with public officials and residents."

It's brought a new vitality and life to the downtown,' said city planner Donald J. Fisher. "it also changed the overall image of the city—which is very hard to do."' Along the Missouri River in Council Bluffs, population 75,000, two riverboat casino resorts recently opened, with each project valued at more than $95 million.

Opening the door to this extraordinary capital investment and more than 2,300 new jobs was the Iowa Racing and Gaming Commission's response to a changing market. Reacting to a regulatory climate that many casino companies found too stifling, the Commission made the adjustments necessary to renew the industry's interest in Iowa.

Unlike Mississippi, where gaming licenses are not limited and the free-market approach creates a tremendously competitive environment, Iowa limits the number of gaming licenses awarded. This approach allows the Commission to control each market and maximize tax revenues. By allowing two riverboat casinos in Council Bluffs and slot machines at the local dog racing track, the Commission has thoughtfully positioned the market to capitalise on the strong population base in the Council Bluffs/Omaha, Nebraska, metropolitan area without creating saturation in the market. Illinois employs the same limited-license approach with similar positive results.

The economic and market dynamics of each state are different, but Mississippi, Illinois and Iowa have all produced overwhelmingly positive results with their respective methods. Generally, emerging jurisdictions have implemented the limited-license approach, but gaming has clearly proven its effectiveness in a variety of different environments. If there is any doubt, simply visit Vicksburg, Joliet or Council Bluffs.

Riverboat gaming

Today, riverboat gambling is a different affair. For instance, the finer 19th-century riverboats had appointments like stained glass windows, chandeliers, and carved, gilded filigree woodwork. In contrast, modern riverboats may appear as quaint on the outside as their predecessors, but the interiors are heavily modernised with sports bars, glitzy Vegas-style decorations, and buffets.

Another big difference is that nowadays the games are run by the house, so gamers play against a corporation. In the old riverboats, the management didn't get involved in the gambling. It wasn't even allowed in some of the boats, but the staff would often turn a blind eye if no other passengers complained.

Dishonest incidents amongst the players occurred, but the reputation of the professional gambler for cheating may be overstated. Punishment for such a travesty could be severe, including whipping and being dropped ashore at the nearest opportunity. Also, the management couldn't necessarily restrain the other passengers from meting out their own punishments. Therefore, the professional gamblers depended on personal skill more than on hidden cards or tricks with mirrors. Games on the old riverboats were limited to cards. Now, you can play such games as slots, video poker, keno, craps, roulette, baccarat, and blackjack.

Rules of gambling riverboats

Riverboat experiences come in many forms. Most gambling riverboats are based on the Mississippi River or one of its tributaries. It's possible to cruise in a boat whose paddles are still powered by steam engines; other boats are permanently moored.

In Missouri, you can find a "boat in a moat," which refers to riverboats that float in dug-out pools that are fed with water from the Missouri River. They are essentially as land-locked as rubberduckies in a tub. The Emerald Queen, a riverboat in Washington State, isn't even in a river. It sits in the Puget Sound, which is part of the Pacific Ocean.

In Nevada, there are at least two riverboats that have been removed from a water environment altogether. They sit-if you'll pardon the simile-like fish out of water. The Mississippi originates in Lake Itasca in northern Minnesota, then flows generally south for 2,470 miles to the Gulf of Mexico. It serves as a border for 10 states. This spread allows ample geographic area to find a riverboat, but it also means that the experience on each may be different, according to the laws of the state in which a boat is located.

Until recently, for instance, the Casino Queen, a riverboat in East St. Louis, Illinois was required by law to engage in river cruises unless restricted by weather or river conditions. Consequently, every two hours, the boat would chug upriver for an hourlong voyage. Recently this requirement was lifted, and it remains moored, open 23 hours a day.

Across the river in Missouri, the President Casino also stays permanently moored. It's housed in the Admiral, an art-deco style riverboat that was used to host cruises earlier in this century. Known for being plush and luxurious, it is noticeably nicer than some boats across the river.

Since the Mississippi bisects the country, riverboat experiences are possible from within many Midwestern states. The boats are especially fun to check out during road trips or when staying in a Midwest city. Gaming riverboats currently operate in Illinois, Indiana, Iowa, Louisiana, Mississippi, Missouri, Nevada, and Washington. It's worth mentioning that riverboats can be experienced without gaming.

The Delta Queen Steamboat Company in New Orleans operates three- to 14-night cruises on their steam-powered paddlewheelers. The Mississippi Queen is outfitted like a cruise liner, including a swimming pool, while the American Queen is outfitted nostalgically, with antiques and old-style grandeur (800-543-7637). Also in New Orleans, the Natchez has nighttime jazz cruises.

The casino market falls into three categories:

— First, there is the 'grind' market, which includes local players who go to the nearest casino or gaming venue;

— secondly, there is the 'tourist' market, which takes in both domestic and international tourists who make a visit to a casino as part of a package that includes other features and trips; and

— thirdly, there is the 'premium' market, which is composed of the big players sometimes called 'high rollers'-who can be either local or international. The casino sector in is extremely competitive in the. Premium market. These high rollers can wager more than US$5 million over just a few' days, and casinos endeavour to attract these players by offering free first-class air travel (or sometimes travel in a private Lear jet), limousines, and accommodation.

Ethical issues related to gambling are important in any assessment of gaming in. One such issue relates to 'problem gamblers'. These people have a gambling habit that has become an obsession, to the extent that they sometimes borrow or even steal to finance their gambling habit. They can neglect their family responsibilities and there have been many instances of parents leaving small children outside casinos or gambling venues while the parent gambles inside.

All casinos recognise these issues and have instituted various responses-including the placing of warnings, the patrolling of car parks, and the establishment of funds for the counselling and support of problem gamblers. Because of these ethical issues, and also because of concerns that organised criminal groups might take control of gambling outlets, all applicants for casino licences have to pass strict criteria and probity checks. All operations, including hotel and club gambling venues, must adhere to detailed regulations.

6

Meeting Industry

A meeting is a planned event in which a group of people gather together to accomplish something. Meetings can be planned in Hotels, cruise ships, convention center, colleges or at several locations by teleconferencing Variable number of people attend meetings depending on the type of meeting Many specialised services technologies and facilities are used at meetings

Meetings industry is also referred to as the MICE industry. Conventions, Expositions, meetings and Incentive travel industry

Kinds of Meetings

Association meetings, Corporate meetings, Trade shows and expositions

Association Meetings

May be made up of trade groups, social groups, Labour Unions, Service associations Generally hold one annual meeting to elect office bearers, plan budgets and activities. Some large associations employ a full time meeting and travel department. Meetings range from 1 day to 1 week. Besides annual meetings there are national regional or international conventions. Annual meetings planned well in advance due to large number of delegates. Proper site selection is vital as Attendance is voluntary Adequate exhibition space is an important planning characteristic. (Depending on the numbers and the events).

Kinds of Corporate Meetings

Management meetings: Largest category in corporate meetings. Financial reviews, strategic planning sessions are held during management meetings.

Training seminars: Ranks second in the number of meetings held. Large companies prefer to take their staff offsite and conduct training sessions.

Sales meetings are essential for teaching new(national 3.6 days 104 attendees; and regional meetings 2.5 days and 42 attendees).

New product introductions (2days, 60 attendees). Professional and technical meetings (2.3 days 62 people) Incentive trips: Offer combination of meeting and recreation Stockholders meetings (1 day, 95 owners attend)

— Decide the Objective: Objective may be business, educational or social. Choose the site as per the objective

— Schedule the meeting : Plan the number of days and the dates when the meeting will be held

— Decide the format: Plan the activities that will take place and the sequence of these activities. Plan thc meals the coffee breaks the timings of the shows etc.

— Choose the location

— Choose the facility: Which hotel, convention centre,

cruise ship would you like to use. Keep the budget in mind while doing this.

Meeting Industry Trends

Meetings come in all shapes and sizes. There are the everyday office meetings, board meetings, seminars -- all the way up to major conferences. And meetings can now be face-to-face, teleconference, videoconference, or online via the Internet. And when is the last time you heard someone say, "Gee, we need to have more meetings." There are more than enough meetings to go around these days, and for a good reason. Meetings are more important than ever. Modern workplaces are built on teams, sharing of ideas, and effective project coordination.

If communication is the lifeblood of any organisation, then meetings are the heart and mind. The place where we communicate the ideas, hash them out, share passion for better or worse, develop new understandings and new directions. It's where deals can happen or fall apart, where strategies are articulated and debated -- in short -- where we engage with others. That's what it's all about, people meeting with people.

Staying Closer to Home

Companies are holding their meetings closer to home as resistance to air-travel continues in the wake of September 11, 2001. Conferees are being offered incentives, by their employers, for driving or taking motor coaches to meeting venues in an effort to avoid travel by air. In some cases, attendees are choosing to drive 6 + hours to attend a meeting in order to avoid flying. Also, many annual company-wide meetings are being split into regional events held closer to home.

Booking Pace – "Short-term becoming even shorter"

Clients are signing meeting contracts at the very last minute, and only after attendance has been confirmed, in order to avoid attrition or cancellation fees. Major annual meetings are now being planned within the year for the year... as budgets are undergoing extreme corporate scrutiny. Additionally, properties continue to cope with sizable cancellations.

Decreasing Meeting Budgets, Meeting Length, Meeting Size

Meeting budgets and programme length continue to be on the decline as companies re-evaluate expenses and suppliers step up the competition for customers, winning business with lower rates. The market today is buyer driven, with planners actively negotiating the very best deal, and looking for added value. For repeat programmes, 2002 budgets are less than that of the year before. Weeklong meetings of the past are currently being reduced to 2-3 days in length. These meetings now have a limit of one banquet or private dining event per conference instead of two or more such events per meeting as was common in previous years.

When dinner or lunch is consumed off site, credits for the meal component of the Complete Meeting Package are more actively requested by planners than was the case previously. Meeting groups have diminished in size – 20-25 persons per conference — although this is not a drastic reduction. Large annual meetings are being split into smaller quarterly meetings.

Third-Party Meeting Planners

Third-party meeting planners continue to manage increasingly more conferences. These planners identify meeting venues, negotiate contracts for space, arrange transportation, schedule theme events and provide entertainment, often attending the meeting as well.

Videoconferencing

This face-to-face meeting alternative seems to have been a reactionary approach following the events of September 11, 2001. Currently, the demand for videoconferencing has tapered off. When this technology is used, it is for smaller groups of less than ten persons.

Meetings being Held Tend to have a Serious Training Component

The vast majority of meetings being held today are serious training sessions. Except for the pharmaceutical industry, very few companies are holding new product introduction or launch sessions. Incentive and weekend meetings have dipped also. The focus of meetings today is on effective training environments — to maximize use of time and the overall meeting investment.

Teambuilding Remains Popular

Even in a slower economy, companies remain willing to invest in creative teambuilding programmes. Demands are for increased innovation in these programmes beyond the traditional high & low rope courses of the past. Unique culinary teambuilding programmes, food & wine tasting sessions, and spa-related events such as reflexology sessions are popular today.

Technology Demands Increase

Demand for use of T-sz1 lines and Internet access remains strong. LCD projectors are essentially standard today and demand for LAN lines to link laptops of all attending participants is increasing. A data port in each meeting room and guestroom is standard today. Many guests, especially from the high-tech industry, are looking for high-speed Internet connections as well. PowerPoint presentations remain commonplace in most meetings. Interesting, low-tech flip charts also remain a very popular tool.

Internet Bookings Rise

The use of the Internet to review meeting venues and to actually book meetings continues to increase each year, with some properties booking 2-3 meetings per month via the Internet. Email usage for requesting and delivering contracts is steadily increasing as well.

Significant Cut Back in Food and Beverage Events

Consistent with decreasing meeting budgets and increasing scrutiny of expenses, there has been a significant cutback in private and themed dinners and private dining events. More than ever before, companies are requiring their conferees to make use of the meal components of the Complete Meeting Package. If a meal is taken off site, properties are being required to provide a meal credit to the Complete Meeting Package for that day.

Growing Source of Hospitality Revenue

Conventions, meetings, and expositions are a major and growing enterprise, not just for the people who work in the business but also for the communities that reap the economic benefits of such meetings. Up to now, however, there has been no way to measure the exact size of the convention business. Some estimates indicate that meetings and conventions increased fourfold in the years between 1980 and 1989, with a full 43 percent increase just from 1987 to 1990. In 1992, the International Association of Convention & Visitor Bureaus (IACVB) employed Deloitte & Youche, a multinational public accounting and consulting firm, to determine a straightforward and statistically valid measure of the economic impact that conventions have on the average city.

Between June 1992 and June 1993, seventy-three cities were the subject of a study involving more than five hundred events worldwide. Deloitte & Touche analysed responses from more than 17,000 meeting delegates, associations, exhibitors, and exposition service contractors before it reached its final conclusions. According to the survey:

— professional and trade associations held 45 percent of conventions;

— 61 percent of the events were international, national, or regional;

— delegates spent an average of $638 for an average stay of 3.48 days;

— out-of-town delegates spent an average of $763, eight times more than local delegates, who spent an average of $93;

— 46 percent of delegate expenditure went to overnight lodging; and

— spending has increased 52 percent from 1985 to 1993.

Certainly, no one who works within the industry would argue with the proposition that the growth and significance of this portion of the hospitality industry has been remarkable. Joseph R. MbGrath, chairman of the

IACVB, sums it up nicely: "The results of this year-long study clearly reflect the substantial economic impact of these events."

Reasons for Growth

No one factor caused the growth of the meetings industry. A number of factors are responsible, but explosive growth in information and easy availability of airline travel head the list.

Information

Perhaps, the primary reason for growth in the industry lies in the major reason people hold meetings, conventions, and expositions: to communicate information. People attend meetings, conventions, and expositions to exchange idea and knowledge. In the last thirty years, availability of information has explored. Computers have made it possible to gather, manipulate, and disseminate a wealth of information on every conceivable subject. Certainly, no one can keep up with all that information. In fact, most people can't keep up with the information in their own field. They attend meetings, conventions, and expositions to learn what's happening in their field, to describe what they are doing, and to trade ideas. This is as true for the hair stylist as it is for the scientist. As more information has become available over the years, it has become necessary to hold more meetings, conventions, and expositions to keep pace.

Airlines

Another major reason for growth in the meetings business is accessibility to air travel. In 1970, the airlines introduced the 747 jumbo-jet, and for the first time large numbers of people could travel from one point to another - no matter how far - quickly and efficiently. Since that time, no destination has been considered "off limits" for the meeting industry, which in turn, has made national and even international meetings, conventions, and expositions possible.

At about this same time, one of the biggest changes between the airline and the meetings business took place - the formation of a trade association called Meeting Planners International (MPI). MPI formed a task force to retain similar privileges of free passage for meeting planners that the major carriers offered travel agents. In the wake of rising fuel costs, the airlines were more than willing to accommodate this new and growing business as a way to increase their passenger load - and their profits.

Besides the introduction of the jumbo jet, the deregulation of the airline industry in the early 1980s also directly effected the meetings business. Deregulation stimulated price wars between airlines, and airfares plummeted, making travel to and from meetings, conventions, and expositions more affordable. As a result, the airlines began catering specifically to the meetings business by offering package deals and negotiated fares. Recently, however, the struggling airline industry changed its policy. Airlines pulled back on special deals, putting planners in the position of demanding - sometimes without success - reduced fares and other perks for meeting attendees. Now, though, things are changing again in the other direction.

Other factors

As the meeting business grew, other businesses,

organisations, and jobs grew to meet its needs, and in turn they made it easier for the meetings business to grow. Specifically, the growth of the lodging industry, convention centers, convention bureaus, conference centers, meeting technology, and the jobs of meeting planner and ground suppliers spurred on and were spurred by the expanding meetings business.

Lodging industry

How has the meetings business affected the lodging industry? To answer that question, it is important to understand the lodging industry in a "before and after" context. "In 1966, group business was a tiny percentage of the total picture for hotels, motels, and resorts," says Mike Leven, at that time president of Days Inns of America (and now president of the Holiday Inn Franchise Group). "In some hotels, group business may account for as much as 80 percent of bookings." As a result of the exceptional increase in the number of meetings and in the tremendous growth in the size of meetings, hotels had to accommodate by becoming physically larger. Consequently, hoteliers of all sizes have adapted their services to variety of clientele, while increasing their profits on this growing segment. Chains such as Sheraton, Hilton, and Hyatt, and later, the Radisson, Omni, and Marriott, cornered the market. Today, these facilities continue to book the majority of the hotel meetings business.

Convention centers

There is another growing niche serving the changing needs of the industry: the convention center. During the past twenty-five years, convention centers have been synonymous with lodging industry expansion. Space, accessibility, and storage facilities have made convention centers a one-stop arena for meetings, conventions, and expositions.

"The days are over when a meeting planner was handed a key to the exhibit hall and told to turn out the lights when he left," says Dan Graveline, director of the Georgia World Congress Center in Atlanta. Convention centers and convention hotels (hotels that include lodging with exhibit and meeting facilities) are now all-inclusive places that have moved beyond the old four-walls, and a ceiling concept of accommodation.

The Coliseum in New York City was probably the first convention center built to accommodate groups of varying size. Completed in 1958, the Coliseum offered flexibility: soundproof movable walls to subdivide large areas, designated registration areas, a variety of lighting options, and truck ramps to the lower exposition floors. Now, hundreds of cities around the world boast their own convention centers. Because of the convention center boom of the last decade or so, many have argued that the market has reached total saturation. Just the same, building continued into the mid-1990s. in the Midwest, existing convention centers in Columbus, Ohio, and Indianapolis, Indiana, added space to expand their facilities.

The Greater Columbus Convention Center doubled in size, adding 216,000 square-foot of exhibit space and a 31,000 square-foot lobby area. The Indiana Convention Center and Hoosier Dome in Indianapolis added a 36,000-square-foot ballroom and 22,050 square feet of flexible meeting space. In 1997, McCormick Place in Chicago dedicated a $675 million addition, making a total of 2.2 million square feet for the entire facility. Cleveland, Ohio, boasts a new center, the Cleveland State Convocation Center, which offer seating for 15,000.

Convention and Visitors Bureaus

Yet another factor affecting the meeting business is the relationship between planners and convention and visitors bureaus (CVBs). According to the IACVB, a convention and visitor bureau is a not-for-profit umbrella organisation that represents a city or urban area in soliciting and serving all types of travelers to that city or area - whether they visit for business, pleasure, or both. In other words, a CVB has three primary purposes:

- — encourage groups to hold meetings, conventions, and expositions in the city or area the CVB represents;
- — assist groups with meeting preparations and offer services during the course of the convention, exposition, or meeting; and
- — encourage tourist to visit and enjoy the historical, cultural, and recreational opportunities that the city has to offer.

CVBs worldwide orient visitors to host cities, act as liaisons between suppliers and meeting planners, and offer convention and meeting management services. CVBs are indispensable in that they attract meetings, conventions, and expositions that might otherwise never be interested in a particular city or region. The task of the CVB is not an easy one. There are unusual requests to fulfill, demands to be met, and schedules to adhere to. Like other segments of the hospitality industry, convention and visitors bureaus face much competition within their segment of the hospitality industry. They, too, must compete regionally, nationally, and internationally for hospitality dollars.

This, however, can be a distinct advantage for the meeting planner. While most CVBs can recommend suppliers, secure hotels, and act as a liaison between a group and the community, they also can provide the meeting planner with materials, tour arrangements, and on-site assistance.

Simply, put, CVBs work for the visitors and meeting planners, as well as for the city - at no cost. (Some are funded solely by membership fees, and others are funded through varying combinations of membership fees, state taxes, and local taxes.) It is important to remember that the meeting planner is the "organiser" and that the CVB is the "assistant." CVBs help visitors learn more about the host city and its area attractions. At the same time, they also help the planner make best possible use of all services and facilities the city has to offer.

Conference Centers

The continued evolution of conference centers has also been greatly influenced by the incredible growth of the meetings business. Formerly, conference centers were usually sparse rooms, barren of everything except chairs and necessary audiovisual equipment. The fitness boom in the 1970s, however, hit even this part of the industry. No longer were conference participants content to sit for hours and hours with no diversion.

Conference centers jumped on the fitness bandwagon and began designing their centers to be more resort-oriented. With recreational and physical exercise facilities available, conference centers now cater to even broader audiences. And they no longer cater to them just on land. Floating conference centers -conference centers aboard ships - are a recent development. Ships are fitted with meeting rooms and auditoriums and offer such technical amenities as closed-circuit television and videoconferencing. Airport meeting rooms are another variation on the theme. American Airlines, for example, provides nineteen conference rooms at O'Hare International Airport.

Not all conference centers are available to the public. Some are owned by corporations and are used only by these corporations. Others, however, are owned by corporations that use the facilities but also rent them out. And still others, owned by universities, are accessible to the public. In fact, Columbia University established the first conference center, Arden House, in Harriman, New York, in 1950.

Use of Technology

The electronics revolution of the last few years has given the meetings and convention industry maximum flexibility with respect to meeting presentations. Videos, 360-degree projection techniques, multi-image presentations, computers, and unique sound system have all become commonplace. Technological advancements within the industry have opened up a world of different ways to communicate that make meetings, conferences, and conventions more interesting to attend and easier to arrange.

Video Technology

Before the mid-1970s, the term "video" was virtually nonexistent. With the advent of such technology as the video projector, video has now become synonymous with the meetings business. There are video-enhanced speakers, multi-image video walls, instant replay, and "live projection." (Live projection is similar to what is now commonly seen at concerts - a close-up of the speaker is projected onto a large video screen, bringing the audience "closer" to the speaker and facilitating a more personal interaction.)

Teleconferencing. In the 1980s, technology advanced beyond video into teleconferencing. Satellites, commonly used to beam news coverage worldwide, made it possible to link separate groups and speakers. In 1980, Holiday Inn broadcast the first national teleconference, linking two thousand participants in thirty-three meeting sites.

Computers. Computers are used in virtually every aspect of the meetings business -including reservations, meeting workshops, and demonstrations. For example, a computerised information network enables CVBs to exchange impotent demographic and historical information on potential meeting sites with other CVBs worldwide. Clearly technology is an indispensable part of the meetings business. Videoconferencing, computer applications, and other technology will continue to advance as quickly as the technological innovations will allow.

Role of the Meeting Planner

The role of the meeting planner began to evolve about twenty years ago and has progressed as the meetings industry has grown. The meeting professional plans and organises the details that make the meeting, convention, or exposition operate smoothly. Certainly no event is produced single-handedly. But without the support of the many planners within the industry, the growth and success experienced by the meetings industry would have come more slowly.

Finally, the arrival of ground suppliers in the 1970s (those who handle details on tours, transportation, sight-seeing, banquets, and hotel registration) began a significant change within the industry. While ground suppliers were primarily "shuttle operators" in the first few years of their existence, they have grown into programme planners offering, for example, special events for spouses of meeting participants, on-site sports tournaments, and motivational speakers. (Meeting planners also can perform these functions.)

Planning and Execution

In its early years, the meetings business suffered growing pains. Many people had no idea of the amount of effort and knowledge required to plan, organise, and execute events. The perception was, and oftentimes still is, that meeting planners are "party-givers." Not so. In one short generation, the field has transformed itself into its own area of specialisation.

What do meeting planners want from property level sales people-the answers may surprise you:

Selection process

How do meeting planners make decisions to locate a destination property for their clients? Relationships are a very important part of the process. The meeting planners indicated that they turn to those with whom they have developed relationships through industry associations such as MPI. They contact their franchise sales representatives and use a local property with a contact that they know to refer them to sister properties within their franchise/management group or contact CVBs.

Online collateral

From these planners, it was clear that they do not have space for vast filing cabinets of meeting planning "kits." I feel vindicated here as I have been advocating electronic brochures that can be downloaded on an "as needed" basis. The other advantages to this approach are that these can be modified as required and are less expensive than printing four-color kits in the thousands that become outdated long before the supply is exhausted. A welldesigned web site including the features that demonstrate a property's functionality for meetings serves as a valuable collateral piece, one that is often accessed before the meeting planner ever approaches the property about a potential client.

Understanding their Needs-Qualifying them

While communication styles vary, it is evident that sales people do not ask them how they would like to be communicated with. Hotel sales people do not ask them what they are looking for in a property-if we did we would discover that it is primarily service and value versus rate.

Franchise meeting planner incentives

This one was a surprise-they do not accept them nor do they use them as a factor in the buying decision. They all felt that to accept such an incentive was to compromise their integrity with their clients.

Consistency in rates across all channels

In the se]lection process, if a property's rates are all over the board, it indicates to the meeting planner that the property is not organised and that when the group is booking, the attendees may be able to find better rates using other channels. When this occurs, the attrition rate goes higher than expected and penalty clauses kick in. To have inconsistent rates across the distribution channels compromises the credibility of the hotel. This is not an exhaustive list but it should give hotel sales departments an indication of what they need to do to maximize their opportunities from third party meeting planners. Before you rush out to develop relationships with every meeting planner on the planet, take the time to qualify them as to the types of meetings they handle, which market segments they specialise in, if any and use your franchise sales contacts. Maximizing opportunities from the sales resources of your franchise is the subject of a whole other newsletter.

The meeting and convention industry has emerged as one of today's most significant sectors of commerce. Crucial to this field are meeting and convention planners, who plan and produce smoothly run conventions, meetings, seminars, and expositions within budget. Meeting Planners, sometimes called Convention Managers, are found both in small companies and in large private corporations, in professional associations, and at visitors and convention bureaus. Some own meeting planning businesses or are employed there as part of a staff.

The work performed by Meeting Planners can be divided into the following responsibilities:

— Programme development
— Marketing and promotion
— Budgeting
— Site selection
— Negotiation
— Travel arrangements
— Entertainment and speakers

— Food arrangements
— Trade show management
— Guest programmes
— Reservations and registration
— Audio-visual equipment
— Public relations
— Programme evaluation

Planners on a large staff for associations and convention bureaus may be assigned one specific aspect of the event such as budgeting or handling reservations and registration, while Planners who work for smaller organisations will often take responsibility for all phases of the event.

In workplaces with several Meeting Planners, three levels of professionalism exist: the Facilitator, the Technician, and the Professional. The Facilitator may be assigned basic tasks such as choosing menus and working with the chosen hotel on a variety of details. This worker is usually concerned with the physical needs of the attendees. The Technician is often responsible for running registration and reservations, selecting and setting up the site, and operating the budget. The Professional designs and sells the event, creates the budget, and oversees all operations. It is this top-level manager who is responsible for achieving the meeting's overall objective: the communication goal of the client.

Meeting Planners working within a corporation have a captive audience; they plan sales and incentive meetings or training seminars for their employees. Planners who represent associations or convention bureaus have the added burden of selling the event and/or location to businesses, associations, and prospective attendees. While Planners for convention and visitors bureaus do not typically organise meetings and conventions for others, they do stage "familiarisation" trips to attract Meeting Planners from associations and corporations to their city.

When marketing is required, Meeting Planners may produce brochures and other publications, handle direct mail operations, and conduct member surveys to help sell and plan association programmes and services. The massive logistical operation of a large convention, trade show or exposition often starts as many as five years before the event. The first step, booking space in halls and hotels, often must be done years in advance. Then, one or two years before the event, Meeting Planners begin developing topics, choosing featured speakers and creating agendas. Much of the work also involves coordinating with other organisations and companies who will present programmes and set up booths. Sometimes hundreds of vendors will exhibit their services or products.

Importants of Skills

Some of the important skills, knowledge, and abilities for Meetings and Convention Planners include the following:

— Coordination - Adjusting actions in relation to others' actions.

— Speaking - Talking to others to effectively convey information.

— Management of Personnel Resources - Motivating, developing, and directing people as they work, identifying the best people for the job.

— Problem Identification - Identifying the nature of problems.

— Implementation Planning - Developing approaches for implementing an idea.

— Active Listening - Listening to what other people are saying and asking questions as appropriate.

— Time Management - Managing one's own time and the time of others.

— Service Orientation - Actively looking for ways to help people.

— Computers - Knowing how to use text and spreadsheet programmes, plus Internet search capability.

7

Hospitality Marketing

Market wisdom today suggests that hospitality companies must embrace technology to compete against traditional competitors, as well as entrants that build their businesses with the latest technology and therefore bear the seal of a new economy entity. In this feverish environment of change, new models of distribution must be designed to lead the charge.

More than any other aspect of business, the Internet revolution is reshaping the concept of the value chain, and how goods and services are distributed to consumers. To grow and succeed, management at hospitality and travel companies of any size must juggle multiple distribution channels, customer segments and intermediaries in their distribution of goods and services. All entities have zeroed in on a business-to-consumer strategy with the intent to influence purchase decisions and own consumer loyalty.

Classic economic models place the producer of goods at one end of the chain and the consumer on the other end, with packaging, shipping, storing and retail middlemen often connecting the two. The Internet, however, has redefined the traditional model and all of the relationships within this value chain. Regardless of whether the good is a product, a service or a combination of the two, the entire consumer purchasing process is undergoing re-evaluation with new business models poised to change or destroy the traditional methods of distribution. Although the hospitality industry began to adopt electronic commerce some 30 years ago when the airline industry developed automated reservation systems, technology is causing massive redesign of product distribution and value creation.

The logical consequence of eDistribution is inescapable: the traditional value chain collapses in what can be described as a "frictionless environment," as suppliers interact directly with consumers through networked technologies. In a frictionless environment, when interaction costs at the margin are close to zero, the cost structure and strategic implications of distribution clearly change very significantly.

In the so-called "old economy," distribution intermediaries existed to compensate for the lack of knowledge on products and pricing, as well as bringing buyer and seller together over a physical distance. As the Internet becomes the ultimate connectivity tool, however, products and services no longer require a physical distribution presence. Intermediaries can continue to contribute to the product or service. But as technology forces out physical inefficiencies in distribution, there are fewer places where middlemen can find safe haven from disintermediation.

The implications of a collapse of the traditional value chain are immense. Because much of the hospitality travel product is experienced-based, the role of distribution can be seen at its simplest as the ability to initiate an experience. Distribution, therefore, becomes part of the product itself. A redefined value chain has both positive and negative implications for each player in the chain. Generally speaking, suppliers benefit from lower distribution costs, better product image control, enhanced brand value and a better relationship with the customer. Intermediaries are likely to experience the greatest short-term turbulence, as each scrambles to assess the value they create and how to sustain it in the value chain. The consumer is most likely to gain, given the opportunity for better service, lower prices, tailored marketing and more options.

Role of Traditional Suppliers

Regardless of distribution method, the products themselves, such as physical guest rooms, airline seats and rental cars, remain largely unchanged in the new economy, although customer information can be used to customize products and services. What is markedly different, however, is an extraordinary increase in competitive pressure to "own" the customer. Since connectivity to the customer is no longer a technology hurdle, each player in the value chain is attempting to develop customer loyalty. Owning or, at a minimum, significantly influencing the channel is an important component of managing customer loyalty.

Numerous supplier limitations have allowed nimble start-ups to take an early lead in the race to influence the consumer purchase decision. Who would have suspected that initially Expedia.com would sell more inventory than the Web sites of some of its suppliers? Most legacy information technology (IT) systems have not been engineered to handle the volume, content and query capabilities required of an online presence in the distribution channel. Customer relationship management (CRM) systems, for example, remain largely in an infancy stage - only the top few percent of frequent hotel guests for example, receive consistent customized service.

Indeed, the vast majority of Web site screens do not mimic how consumers buy hospitality and travel products and services. To secure a hotel booking online, for example, the customer typically enters an arrival date and length of stay. In reality these variables often are influenced by price, but this symbiotic relationship is not well represented at Web sites. Web sites will clearly need to provide more information and suggestions for customized and packaged travel if they are truly to serve the interests of travelers.

Consider the major issues for each of the key suppliers:

Airlines

The airlines have continued to be leaders in a shortening value chain by eliminating activities that do not add value, while developing such items as electronic ticketing and last-minute fares at low prices. Recently, five major airlines have announced they plan to create a megasite for eDistribution, a plan that responds to the threat of online travel agencies as they attempt to reintermediate themselves with customers. Whereas the airlines previously did not distribute their products directly to consumers, the new economy is requiring them to collaborate with their historical competitors with strategies to own the customer.

Hotel Companies

Channel conflict continues to be a significant issue among hotel companies. The price of a physical hotel room often varies widely depending on the source of booking (e.g., call center, Internet travel site, retail travel agency, corporate agent or direct contact with the property). Even though "single-image" inventory is widely favored in the industry, displaying the same image to all potential buyers remains challenging and is largely unfulfilled. Legacy reservation systems were not designed for true single image inventory. With available technology moving the industry toward price transparency, companies will feel intense pressure to compete on brand and differentiation, rather than price alone. Hotels must also manage additional customer touch points, an activity that is not always successful in the physical world. Guest recognition and tailored service are hallmarks of excellent properties. Customer relationship management is powered by good data, however, which remains a rarity within the hotel community. Extending recognition and consistency of service to the Internet and new sales channels compounds the problem of effectively managing the entire guest experience.

Traditional Intermediaries

Changes brought by eDistribution have had the most profound effect on players that are positioned between suppliers and consumers in the distribution chain. These intermediaries are going through a period of transformation in how they do business:

Travel Agents: The retail travel agent is the best-known intermediary in the hospitality industry. A portion of a retailer's activities today remains value-added, while other roles are "old economy" in nature and becoming obsolete. The act of printing and issuing paper airline tickets is rooted in history when only Global Distribution System (GDS) terminals provided inventory access, and airlines required paper tickets for accounting. An area where travel agents do continue to add tremendous value is in advising travelers of destinations, tailoring travel to individual preferences, and saving time and money for the traveler before and during the trip. The new role for this group is that of knowledge manager.

Tour Operators: These intermediaries are also at significant risk from the collapse of the hospitality and travel value chain, as the Internet introduces new forms of competition. Tour operators aggregate travel products and repackage those products under a brand name. Tour operators in Europe own a much larger portion of the leisure travel market than in North America, with several large players dominating approximately half of the market. In the United States and Canada, the tour business is extremely fragmented, with few well-known brands and thin profit margins. Suppliers connected with consumer groups have the potential to mimic and exceed the purchasing power of individual tour operators. What prevents well-branded airline, hotel, and car rental companies from agreeing to share inventory and creating their own packages? Nothing - as is the case with many packages offered today by airlines and hotel companies. Furthermore, customer loyalty is often stronger with the travel agent that sells packages in North America.

Immense business and technology issues also exist for tour operators seeking to function in the new economy. Call centers create an artificial demand regulator, limiting the amount of product available on a free-sale basis by the number of agents answering calls. If the same model and IT systems are opened to Web traffic, a virtually unlimited amount of demand could overwhelm free-sale and price-yielding techniques that are designed for a different business model. To compete, tour operators will need to use networking tools and offer complete excursions that are priced in real-time and tailored to their customers.

GDS and Switches GDS providers offer some of the most reliably engineered IT transaction systems in existence. In a frictionless environment, however, Internet connectivity could ultimately eliminate the need for the GDS. GDS providers are now powering many of the virtual travel agent and online supplier bookings, and are demonstrating that intermediaries can still play an effective role by delivering reservation capabilities faster and cheaper than individual suppliers on their own.

The fact that the GDS and switching organisations such as THISCO and Wizcom are still used to book online travel indicates that new entrants have eliminated only a part of the traditional hospitality and travel value chain. Some friction in distribution still exists when these intermediaries are used to gain access to supplier inventory.

New dot.com Intermediaries

Virtual travel agents represent a new form of intermediary, with some estimates placing the number of Web sites with travel booking capabilities at close to 1,000. Virtual travel agents charge a commission from suppliers (about 5 percent for hotels), but typically offer a lower flat fee for airlines. Many of these companies will clearly have to revisit their Internet strategies and business models over the next several years, as hotels, airlines and other suppliers become more aggressive in offering consumers direct access to inventory. Many of these new dot.com companies have yet to be profitable and are running out of time and money to gain significant market share to offset high costs in technology and payroll.

New intermediaries such as Priceline.com have used the Internet to create a demand collection system. Worldres.com has amassed a central inventory of more than 11,000 properties, of which many are bed and breakfasts and vacation rentals that could not conform to the GDS listing requirements. A large number of additional entrants are expected in this arena in the next twelve months, particularly in the business-to-business arena, allowing corporations of all sizes to more effectively buy travel products.

Consumers

With the restructuring of the value chain, consumers stand

to gain the most. Whether consumers choose to book online, or use the Internet for research and a physical travel agent to book, the level of knowledge, choices and convenience is unprecedented. The purchase experience will only improve as broadband access and multimedia content are married with product availability and one-to-one marketing activities. Distribution costs are eliminated when a value chain is shortened, and many of these savings are passed on to consumers in the form of bonus miles, last-minute fares and Web-direct-only pricing.

Vast amounts of information and the intensity of advertising "noise" can clearly be overwhelming to many consumers. But as the ease of use and customised offerings improve under the banner of powerful brands, the superiority of eBusiness applications for the hospitality and leisure industry will eventually become the norm. At that point, the new economy will no longer be "new," and the value chain will reflect the power of the Internet and its global networking capabilities.

Revenue Management Strategy

A revenue management strategy that incorporates all of the revenue drivers such as GDS, the web site and the electronic distribution channels is key. However, it requires the involvement of the sales department and all other profit centers of the hotel. This is unlike a budget in that a revenue strategy is renewable and adjustable where a budget is usually written in stone.

A sound revenue management strategy includes the optimum revenue mix and the tactics to achieve it — this is where the marketing plan comes in! "Managing" revenue is just that — it assumes an element of control in the revenue that you accept from various sources based upon cost of reservation, commissions, etc. A revenue management strategy establishes "target" numbers to be achieved through a variety of ways; sales, manipulating the GDS, controlling the allocation and rate in the electronic distribution channels, etc. In other words, it is a pro-active rather than reactive function that simply turns the faucets on and off.

The sales strategies in the marketing plan flow from the revenue management strategy although sales is critical in developing it. The sales department is critical in that they have their fingers on the pulse of the market. They are responsible for assembling the economic information on market conditions and analysing the potential threats to the market as well as identifying the opportunities. The sales department knows the potential of each market segment and the rate that each one will bear.

The development of the revenue management strategy allows sales to gage how many rooms in a given period they can book by market segment and at what rate. It also insures that existing and future group blocks won't be sabotaged by lower rates on the web site or distribution channels.

How exactly should this process work?

— *Gathering the info*: Each member of the team, but especially sales, should have been keeping information in regard to the market such as trends indicated by the STR reports and other industry sources. Sales should take the temperature of top accounts to see what their forecasts for travel next year look like. The group logs pace reports for this year and next year should also be put into the file. Sales should also have the situation analysis completed as well as identified challenges and opportunities for the upcoming year.

— *Analysing the Revenue Data:* The revenue reports should be analysed to indicate the percentages currently generated by all revenue drivers. This, of course assumes that the data is accurate. If anyone has any doubts about the importance of proper market segment coding by reservations and the front desk they should end here. It is "GIGO" (garbage in — garbage out)! If there aren't accurate numbers, you will be playing a SWAG game.

— *The Facilitation*: This is the meeting of the minds, GM, sales, reservations and any other interested party such as the owner. They take a look at the budget, market conditions, all sources of revenue, etc. and begin projecting the revenue strategy by segment. This can be a contentious process as the sales department fights for accounts and room allocations by rate. However, as an associate once said, harmony is vastly overrated. This process can take several days as all of the evidence is presented and numbers are plugged into the model and adjusted — yada, yada. It never hurts to have an outside consultant facilitate this process to provide objective third party input.

— *The Final Product*: The spreadsheet, created from compromise that fulfills the requirement of the budget, becomes the basis of the revenue strategy. Every revenue driver is identified and the ideal mix of revenue and rate is there to yield the targeted REVPAR. Every revenue driver in the revenue strategy should have its own strategy and tactics section in the marketing plan — including the web site, the GDS strategy and the electronic distribution channels.

— *The Review Process*: The same fractious group that designed the strategy should meet periodically, it could be monthly or quarterly, to make adjustments based upon reality. In the initial development, "triggers" should have been identified that would automatically call for adjustments. Those triggers include unanticipated market changes, good or bad, changes in the economy and any national security breaches.

Use of Trade-Outs

There is a common arrangement in the hotel business where the hotel receives goods and/or services in exchange for rooms, food, and/or beverages. Overwhelmingly, trade-out is used to purchase advertising.

Keep in mind the following points when doing trade-outs:

— The hotel is still the buyer and the advertising source is still the vendor. The only difference is the method of payment for the advertising. Instead of money, you are paying with goods and services.

— The contract should include the provision that the vendor is not to receive any portion of the rooms, food, or beverage until that amount of advertising has already been received. This is not barter; the hotel has purchased advertising and should not pay for anything it has not received.

— There should be an expiration date for the validity of the trade out (usually six to nine months). Clearly, the shorter, the better.

— The contract should exclude certain dates from availability, both for rooms, food, and beverage. Clearly, blackout all possible or close to sellout dates for rooms, among others. Also, exclude high traffic holidays from food and beverage such as Mothers Day, Valentine's Day, etc.

— The contract should specify the exact dollar value for each room, food, and beverage which they will receive, each good and service itemized. In addition, it is important to consider not giving dollar for dollar exchanges.

The Director of Sales, in conjunction with Accounting, should determine the actual cost of what the hotel is exchanging for the advertising as the required analysis into whether or not to execute this arrangement.

For instance, the cost of providing one room night with a rack rate of $100.00 is different than the cost of providing one dinner priced at $100.00. Faced with costs of 25% in the Rooms Department versus 85% in the Food Department, the actual cost of giving them away is dramatically different. This analysis should be done prior to the execution of the contract.

Always separate the proportion of rooms, food, and beverage being exchanged and allocate a cost to each.

It is best to look at the average of the prior three months' expenses in each department, bearing in mind the time of year in which the vendor will be consuming the services to adjust these costs appropriately. After the contract has been executed, Accounting should be given a copy of the cost calculations attached to a copy of the contract.

Record-keeping

When accounting receives an "invoice" for the advertising which has run, it is essential not to enter this into Accounts Payable.

Some vendors issue an actual invoice for the retail price of the advertising and those invoices can accidentally get entered into Accounts Payable. Because we have received the advertising, we have incurred a liability, but not a cash liability. The vendor is now free to consume rooms, food, or beverage according to the terms of the contract. However, this liability does not belong in Accounts Payable and it is essential to keep all trade-out balances in a separate account which can be monitored separately from other payables.

Accounting should retrieve the contract from the files and determine the cost of the advertising which has been received on the basis of the proportion of rooms, food, and beverage in the arrangement. Assign a dollar amount of actual cost for the invoice to be written down to. The amount of advertising received must be determined either from the vendor or from the contract in order to assign the hotel's cost. The first entry at the left illustrates how to enter the invoice easily and correctly.

Accounting

When the vendor has consumed the rooms, food or beverage, the vendor should sign for the services on the folio or check and it should be treated as other receivables. However, during the night audit or reconciliation process, this revenue and the settlement need to be adjusted off. The steps for this depend upon your accounting system; that applies to the final entry necessary to complete this transaction, as illustrated in the second entry in the gray box. Of course, the final entry depends on exactly what was consumed by the vendor in order to determine the allocation to the departments.

The foregoing entry provides both for the Accounting Department to ensure proper allocation and accounting of this transaction and for the relevant department incurring the actual cost of the advertising to be relieved of the costs and their impact on the departmental profit and percentages. If the departments are not receiving any revenue from these guests or patrons, they should be credited with the associated costs. This transaction is to reduce advertising expense and Sales & Marketing should incur the total cost of this transaction.

A final and very important point: consult with your Certified Public Accountant, lawyer or other competent professional before implementing any procedure like this.

Tax laws change frequently and taxes, particularly sales taxes, may be impacted. Neither the author nor this publication assume any responsibility for the consequences of using these procedures and do not intend to set policies and/or procedures for individual properties or the hotel industry.

Urban Timeshare in Hospitality Industry

Urban timeshare has inspired intense interest during the past two years with forecasts that it will be a new wave of product in a growing industry. Yet the record speaks to a slow start for this sector. The timeshare industry at large has continued to thrive with growth posted at 16 percent annually in sales volume since 1980. Operators have found the industry resilient to both economic and lodging downturns. High returns and growth opportunities are forecast for both hotels and independent operators with the industry's credibility and opportunities on the rise as reputable developers join the sector. The latest high-profile entrant promises to aid consumers in evaluating alternative products. Thomas Cook, the giant travel company, has announced it will represent high-quality timeshare properties. The entry of this well known name offers a significant boost for all reputable timeshare businesses.

Even with the strength of the timeshare industry generally, development of urban timeshare projects has lagged To date, just three urban developments are creating a standard The Manhattan Club in New York, Marriott's Custom House resort in Boston; and The Edinburgh Residence in Scotland. Urban timeshare would appear to offer distinct advantages to the hospitality industry, but it has yet to be developed to any great degree by companies. A combination of market forces and industry challenges have created short-term hurdles. The long-term prognosis, however, may offer opportunities for developers in a niche sector attracting sophisticated, upscale buyers, who are interested in the urban experience.

One of the major advantages timeshare products offer hospitality groups is the resilience of the sector to economic downturn. With the exception of a small decline in sales volumes in 1985, American Resort Development Association (ARDA) statistics suggest that timeshare sales have survived the peaks and troughs characterising the hospitality industry Timeshare occupancy tends to be more predictable, and the manager of the timeshare units finds it far easier to manage variable costs, particularly labour, than his or her counterpart in the hotel business. Despite the undisputed interest of almost all major hospitality groups, however r, only Marriott has made a large-scale commitment to the concept outside the United States.

The initial economics of urban timeshare look beguiling to a developer. The average cost of development of a five-star London hotel room can be anything up to £225,000 per room (when an existing property is converted). For a 300-room hotel, this brings the development price to £67.5 million. After adding 10 percent uplift for additional facilities to be offered, the total product cost would amount to approximately £74.25 million. Consider the economic return if that same project were developed as a timeshare. Assuming a sales price of approximately £17,500 per week, and 50 weeks of occupancy per year, total income would amount to £262.5 million. On this basis, sales of just 15 weeks of inventory would fully cover the product cost. Assuming administrative/overhead costs of 10% (i.e., approximately £26 million), our hypothetical urban timeshare would yield a staggering £162 million (62 percent of the total cost) to cover sales and marketing expenses, and profits.

The "numbers" are clearly tantalising. Two key reasons, however, have mitigated against urban timeshare;

— the increased profile and attractiveness of timeshare has coincided with a property boom in the major cities; and

— inability to control marketing costs.

In the London market, for example, many developers and botchers alike have considered the viability of timeshare, either on a stand - alone basis or as a mixed-use plan. Property prices have escalated over the past few years, however. At the same time, the return that can be generated from other options (such as serviced apartments) has been sufficiently high to discourage companies from developing an urban timeshare, particularly with the additional risk associated principally with the marketing costs.

Resort timeshares have been successful, in part due to differential pricing and high occupancy rates achieved throughout the year as a result of an attractive climate and a variety of recreational amenities. Likewise, urban timeshare must also be based in locations that can attract visitors throughout the year. In the case of city sites, customers also include corporations. which may buy blocks of weeks. For these reasons, areas just outside New York, London and Paris have been regarded as the most attractive locations.

The New York Manhattan Club is perhaps the best example of this type of development. Developed by the Eichner family, which builds and owns retail, commercial and residential properties, The Manhattan Club offers high specification suites with an average size of 650 square feet. The original sale price of $15,000 per week has climbed to $21,000. The site actually opened in August, 1997, and to date approximately 16 percent (i.e., 3,000 weeks) have been sold out of a total 18,000 weeks. The total site cost $60 million, of which half has been made available to timeshare, and the refurbishment of the timeshare element is estimated at $70 million. Approximate revenues to date based on 3,000 weeks sold at an average price of $15,000 amount to some $45 million, which provides very substantial cash flow to finance the continuing development. Multiple weeks have been sold to corporations for use by company employees. Surprisingly, sales to individuals are typically made to people living within a 90-minute radius of New York. Heavily used by owners, opportunities for exchanging into The Manhattan Club are fairly limited, although it is affiliated to the RCI exchange network.

The Edinburgh Residence in Edinburgh, Scotland, represents one of the best examples of urban timeshare outside the United States. Three directors, all of whom had previously worked in the timeshare business, set up the Edinburgh Residence project. These individuals recognised the gap in the market for flexible urban timeshares, which could exploit the "short break" market. Edinburgh represents a fairly unusual location for European urban timeshares because it does not typically offer the corporate customer potential of cities such as New York, London or Boston. Occupancy is smoothed throughout the year using the RCI exchange, with approximately 10 percent of clients taking advantage of the exchange programme.

Financing Issues

Once a timeshare site is identified, financing becomes a major issue. particularly for companies that are not well established. There is still widespread institutional anxiety among finance providers for timeshare developments. Those developers able to obtain development finance generally have an existing relationship with the institution and a track record in timeshare / timeshare sales. In this regard, distribution capacity is regarded as key. The timeshare developer must have a sound business plan with a focus on, and substantiation of, the projected sales volumes. Extensive due diligence is carried out, usually both by the developer and the institution. Moreover, large projects ($50 million +) are preferred to smaller projects. Depending on the structure of the timeshare development, there may be additional security required.

In the United States, only a few institutions will participate in timeshare financing. There are three or four specialist lenders, of which the most notable is Finova. Those lenders specialising in financing will provide the construction loan principally to secure the provision of consumer financing. In the United kingdom and Europe, banks and credit institutions generally lend only to timeshare on the back of existing relationships. Many of the high street banking names are reluctant to provide loans to the industry, although specialist finance providers are beginning to appear. Finova now has a European presence, for example. Construction finance for the new players is still very difficult.

The Edinburgh Residence was an exception to this rule. One-third of the financing was provided by 3i (Glasgow) and Aberdeen Asset Managers (U.K. venture capitalists), while two-thirds came from the Royal Bank of Scotland. Agreeing the funding for the project is regarded as the biggest single achievement of the project directors and is largely attributed to finding the right people. The refurbishment of the Edinburgh Residence was done successfully, and confidence amongst the finance providers has accordingly grown. The first 10 suites of The Edinburgh Residence were opened on February 1, 1997. Royal Bank of Scotland then accelerated the funding so that all 30 of the suites were opened by late July, 1997.

Marketing and Sales

In many respects, marketing and sales costs are the "great unknown" as regards timeshare in general, but more particularly urban timeshare. where there is far less experience on which accurate predictions can he made. The average active project reports marketing and sales costs of 38.5 percent, although 48.2 percent of projects have marketing and sales costs of more than 40 percent. Moreover, the three major urban timeshares have unique profiles. The marketing programme of Marriott's Custom house in Boston is highly developed, for example, as one of a number of timeshare developments owned by the hotel company.

When a project is confined to a single site, the marketing of an urban timeshare development is a much more difficult problem. The key issue is balancing the need to generate leads and achieve a high conversion rate, whilst minimising marketing costs. The Manhattan Club, for example, sends targeted mailings through credit card companies, and advertises in publications such as theatre brochures and broadsheets. The timeshare achieves a 20-25 percent conversion rate with 400-500 families visiting the site a week. The Edinburgh Residence, on the other hand, uses a third-party company to do its marketing. Like The Manhattan Club, it relies on direct mail and displayed advertisements in the broadsheets. However, it also gains a substantial proportion of its customers through in-house affinity relationships in the form of promotional deals. Its total marketing costs amount to only 18 percent of the cost base, which is substantially lower than the industry as a whole. Conversion rates are approximately 30 percent, in contrast to the average market rare of approximately 15 percent.

Maintenance Fees

In the recent RCI consulting study on the resort timeshare industry in the United States, average maintenance fees ranged from $270 for a studio unit to $425 for a three bedroom unit with an overall weighted average of $360 per week. The maintenance fee for both The Manhattan

Club and the Custom House development is $575 per week, or approximately $82 a night. This is clearly at the top end of the market. The Edinburgh Residence's annual maintenance fee, on the other hand, at £195 per week per annum is regarded as inexpensive by approximately 95 percent of the clients, according to management. At approximately £28 per day, this is certainly towards the lower end of expectations. As yet, maintenance fees in general do not seem to reflect the added advantage which timeshare providers should achieve from the ability to manage costs better. With the increased transparency in the market produced by initiatives such as the Thomas Cook entry, competition to keep down maintenance fees is expected to increase.

Developments

The Thomas Cook entry into the timeshare market is undoubtedly the most significant development in timeshare in recent years. The company announced at the beginning of June that a number of its sales outlets would represent four-star and above-quality properties built by reputable developers. Thomas Cook retail outlets are expected to offer a range of timeshare, although the company's role is understood to be one of marketing rather than closing sales. The advantage to the consumer should be the increased transparency of products offered by developers. Previously, potential customers have had to do their own research. From a developer's point of view, there are a number of attractions.

A customer entering the process through Thomas Cook may be more favourably predisposed toward the product. This may improve conversion ratios compared to the typical customer who has responded to a direct marketing initiative. For those high quality developers that have only one or two sites, it should help to alleviate the need for an expensive marketing team whilst benefiting from the economies of scale which Thomas Cook can achieve by marketing several different projects. In addition, Thomas Cook obviously has the ability to arrange flights and rental cars to transport people to the Site without the need to involve an additional party. Overall, this should help reduce the administrative costs incurred by the developer.

Urban timesharing may be slow to get off the ground, but it still offers great potential. Once property prices begin to soften in major cities, the industry can expect more entrants into urban timeshare. For high -quality developments in Europe, Thomas Cook should have a positive impact on individual ownership of both resort and urban timeshare. It is likely, however, that the urban timeshare purchaser will be a more sophisticated upscale buyer. The surprising trend seen in the up-market developments to date is the attraction they have held for people within a relatively short radius of the metropolitan centre. Once more up-market urban timeshare becomes available, this trend is likely to be less marked.

Notwithstanding the potential attractiveness of urban timeshare to individuals, the real breakthrough is likely to come as more corporations become buyers of timeshare weeks. This is likely to occur when the cost of acquiring and maintaining an urban timeshare compares more favourably with the cost of hotel rooms, when corporate discounts are taken into account. With increased transparency of costs and better yield management, which timeshare developers should be able to achieve, a gradual decline in the annual maintenance fee is anticipated. Once this occurs, and developers are able to provide satisfactory quality assurance, interest is likely to grow in the corporate market. As the resale market in such property develops, this should also enhance interest. particularly if the timeshare weeks hold their price.

Hospitality Marketing Challenges

The current economic slowdown represents a major challenge for the hospitality industry. Many hotels and restaurants have weathered the storm by slashing budgets, laying off employees, and reducing guest amenities. Although these tactics have allowed the hospitality industry to stem its short-term losses, they are not long-term solutions.

In response to this challenge, more hotels and restaurants have turned to Internet-and network-enabled business solutions. In the United States, for example, a 2001 National Restaurant Association survey revealed that more than half of all restaurant operators now access the Internet for business-related purposes, including marketing, training, and communications. In the hotel industry, in-room amenities such as high-speed Internet access and video-on-demand have become must-have items for business travellers. Wireless networks also play an increasingly vital role, linking together everything from point-of-sale terminals to housekeeping and security management systems.

As a result of these innovations, the hospitality industry has discovered that it is possible to cut labour and overhead costs without sacrificing product quality or customer service. These solutions are relevant to hospitality-related businesses of every size, from single-unit operations to multinational corporations. According to the US National Restaurant Association, the U.S. restaurant industry in 2001 suffered its slowest sales growth in a decade, and 2002 sales growth will remain below average. The hotel industry in the United States suffered an even more dramatic decline; average room occupancy rates in late 2001 dropped by as much as 30 to 40% before recovering somewhat during the first months of 2002.

According to Barry Goldstein, a strategist for the Cisco Systems Internet Business Solutions Group, recent improvements in the industry's fortunes come with a caveat: Among hotels in the United States, the recovery is happening at lower price points-an average of 25% lower. "Hotels must find a way to drive additional customer revenue while increasing employee productivity," Goldstein says.

Restaurants face a similar dilemma. In addition to building customer demand for high-margin menu items, restaurant operators must manage food and overhead costs more carefully than ever before. Achieving these goals, in turn, requires operators to track inventories, food use, payroll, and other key metrics as accurately as possible-an especially difficult task for geographically dispersed, multi-unit operations.

The hotel industry faces additional problems maintaining established revenue sources. Income from guest phone calls, for example, has declined substantially as more travelers use wireless phones. According to Goldstein, one major hotel chain expects a $90 million shortfall in phone-related revenue, reflecting a continuing long-term decline in a major source of income for large and small hotel operators alike. "The question is," Goldstein says, "how do you make up that difference with revenue from other sources?"

Hospitality businesses also face constraints on their ability to apply traditional network-enabled business solutions:

— Hotel and restaurant chains often include multiple business units, widely scattered across the United States and around the world.

— Expensive, time-consuming, and disruptive physical infrastructure upgrades are not an option for many hotels and restaurants.

— Hotel and restaurant employees are highly mobile, work irregular hours, and rarely have access to traditional offices and computers.

— Technological solutions must enhance opportunities to provide "high-touch," personalised customer service-not replace them.

Variety of Network-enabled Solutions

Restaurants and hotels can now choose from a variety of network-enabled solutions tailored to meet their business needs. These technologies emphasize speed and flexibility; work well with a distributed, mobile workforce; and leverage existing infrastructure and business methods. Examples of these technologies include:

— Wireless local-area networks

— Internet-based e-learning tools

— Web-based hosted applications

— Broadband Internet access

— Voice over Internet Protocol services

— Virtual private network technology

When applied to the hospitality industry, these technologies offer a variety of compelling business solutions:

— Wireless point-of-sale systems that keep restaurant servers on the floor, streamline the order-taking process, and minimize mistakes

— E-learning applications that allow hospitality employees to receive on-demand training, regardless of where or when they work

— A new generation of revenue-generating guest services, including broadband Internet access, video-on-demand, and Internet-enabled telephony systems

— Web-based profit-and-loss accounting, invoicing,

payroll, and point-of-sale systems that link to enterprise systems at corporate headquarters and reduce technology overhead costs at individual business units

— Kitchen management systems that use the Internet to communicate with vendors and suppliers, automatically scheduling food orders, updating inventories, and even tracking food safety data

Benefits

Many of these solutions deliver quantifiable results; according to one study, wireless point-of-sale systems in a full-service restaurant can increase service speed 20 to 30% while dramatically decreasing waste-related food costs. Other quantifiable benefits from employing Internet-based and network-enabled applications include:

— Lower labour costs and higher productivity—According to Joe Skorupa, editor of Hospitality Technology magazine, a wireless point-of-sale system in a full-service restaurant makes it possible for fewer servers to generate more per-customer revenue. "High-margin items like desserts and beverages require up-selling," Skorupa says, "and that requires the servers to spend more time interacting with customers."

— Reduced infrastructure upgrade costs—Cisco long-reach Ethernet technology allows hotels to provide broad-band Internet access and related services via existing phone lines-potentially saving thousands of dollars in cabling and other infrastructure upgrade expenses. Wireless networks extend connectivity to both guests and staff in areas where wiring isn't available, such as hotel lobbies or meeting rooms. Wireless networks at the front door enable mobile check-in services, improving both employee productivity and customer satisfaction.

— Streamlined business operations—The flow of information between business units and corporate headquarters can create a costly bottleneck for multi-unit hotels and restaurants. Web-based applications eliminate this problem, giving managers immediate, detailed access to any operating unit's profit-and-loss statements, payroll, inventory, and other vital data.

As Steve Nye, general manager of the Cisco Building Broadband Solutions unit, notes, these technologies provide other benefits that may be hard to quantify but are vital nevertheless. "Hotels see [Internet access] as part of their competitive advantage; it puts people in the rooms and boosts occupancy rates, creating other revenue opportunities," he says. Nye adds that many business travelers now view such amenities as a "check-off" item when they select a hotel; as a result, properties that can't offer such services will lose business to those that do.

The benefits of Internet connectivity and related technologies are not limited to large, multi-unit hospitality operations. A single-unit full-service restaurant, for example, can benefit from a wireless point-of-sale solution that improves staff communication and cuts labour costs.

Advocacy in Hospitality Marketing

Most hospitality marketers recognize the importance of advocacy— word of mouth referrals—in fuelling demand for their travel and tourism products. Referrals are the highest-ranked source of information consumers use to select travel services, according to a 1998 report by the Travel Industry Association of America. Even academic studies have confirmed the important role of word of mouth. However, the same studies also conclude that marketers must invest more heavily in magazines, television, newspapers and travel agencies; that they're not doing enough in those areas to maximize promotion of their operations and thus gain significantly more business.

A high percentage of sales come from word of mouth, yet according to these studies, travel marketers are not doing enough mass marketing? If referrals from satisfied customers represent the most successful avenue to attracting new clients, does it make sense for the marketers to send almost all their budgets in another direction, toward on mass marketing channels? This view is misguided when it encourages marketers to hurl hundreds upon thousands of dollars at conventional communications channels despite common knowledge and clear evidence that certain less conventional alternatives, i.e., word of mouth techniques, have been shown to be far more cost-effective and promise greater returns.

Could travel marketers then do a better job attracting new customers, and keeping "old" customers coming back, if more budgets were directed toward enhanced word-of-mouth programmes? The research seems to conclude so, suggesting that a comparatively smaller investment in "customer advocacy" marketing can be expected to yield a higher return on investment dollars. Although it's certainly true that word of mouth can't do it all by itself, this avenue is typically vastly over-looked for its power to do what it can.

In today's marketing environment, in fact, travel firms attempting to reach target consumers through traditional brand-building approaches, such as advertising and customer-loyalty programmes, face higher hurdles than ever before. Advertising, increasingly cluttered, typically produces low levels of trust, and in many categories fails to provide true product differentiation.

With the array of media choices increasing continually—think cable, the Internet, elevator ads—advertising messages now reach smaller and smaller audiences. Though many customer-loyalty programmes have proven highly effective for the frequent business traveller, the same cannot be said for most other segments of the travel industry. Few families, for example, return to the same resort over and over again or take the same cruise more than once.

Advocacy-focused strategy

The challenge then presented by the dynamics in today's travel marketplace is to develop ways to strategically leverage the power of referrals on a grand scale, producing a demonstrable return on marketing investment. In an effective customer-referral strategy, for example, an experienced, satisfied guest informs friends and relatives not only about the great experience but also about nuts-and-bolts details about the travel firm's menu of services. This is accomplished by giving the satisfied guest some kind of "tool" to educate him/her properly. Such tools are designed to steer customer "advocates" toward relating their experiences not just with enthusiasm but with genuine knowledge as well.

This combination of facts-and-experience spurs customers to advocate not just once but again and again. We humans after all tend to trust our messengers. If even one friend, colleague, relative tells you she had a great time at a resort or on a cruise, you tend to believe her and will likely catch the fever for going out and experiencing this great getaway yourself! Consider how powerfully this "advertising message" might cut through the clutter and clamor of TV and radio commercials, Sunday circulars, junk mail, what have you.

Consider this success story: A cruise line had come to realise that, though customer advocacy played a pivotal role in its success as an industry leader, it nonetheless possessed no hard information on how critical it had been in terms of actual customer purchasing decisions or direct financial impact. Additionally, management decided (on a hunch) that the only ways to significantly increase advocacy were to either "bribe" customers by providing them with a monetary or credit incentives, or seek ways to make the cruise line's satisfied customers even more thrilled in hopes they would then share their "delight" with others.

Upon further reflection, however, neither option appeared very attractive. The first one, incentives, held the potential to undermine the company's premium brand position. Since the brand's foundation is built on the promise of "reliability," "integrity," "leadership" and "product innovation," it could be argued that bribing customers with an incentive would be at odds with the brand's core value. Encouraging advocacy via a monetary incentive might send the wrong message.

The second, the "customer delight" strategy, held limited appeal as well. Under this approach, the company's representatives would attempt to systemically exceed customers' service expectations, a strategy that sounded good in theory but in practice would surely increase costs per customer, perhaps to a level out of balance with potential returns. Then too was the risk that the many, now more, expensive "delighted customers" would still not bother to share their delightful experiences with others, despite added efforts on the part of the company.

So the company chose to investigate what other measurable, cost-effective methods it could employ to encourage customers to advocate its services. Its first step was to fully understand the value of an advocate. Based on previous industry research, they knew that:

— Receiving a recommendation from a customer advocate increased a prospect's purchase probability by 18 percent.

— On average, each advocate made three unique recommendations annually.

— The average purchase of those who had been advocated to was $650.

— As a result of the above, each advocate could be said to be worth approximately $400 in additional annual revenue.

— Further analysis revealed that an increase in the advocacy rate company-wide by only five percent would produce $240 million in new revenues.

With such data in hand, the company faced a challenge: Could it implement a strategy that systematically increased advocacy rates among its customer base? Also, how could it verify that such a strategic investment would be worth the effort?

To find out, a market research experiment was designed involving customers who had recently taken week long cruises. These purchasers were randomly assigned to a control or one of two test groups. Test Group A received a standard, off-the-shelf promotional-product type loyalty gift. Test Group B got a gift video designed to highlight and explain the uniqueness and value of the product. This inherent "customer education" subtly encouraged and "trained" the purchasers in Test Group B how to talk more knowledgeably about the product. Those in the control group received no post-purchase gift at all.

At the end of the three-month test period, research showed that the cruise company could expect dramatic differences in behaviour among the three groups. The control group showed no change from previous customer testing and Test Group A, the one that got the off-the-shelf gift, acted no different from the control group. However, Test Group B exhibited a remarkable increase in advocacy, demonstrating to the company that it could in fact proactively increase advocacy rates to great advantage. In terms of cost effectiveness, quantification of the purchase behaviour reported an 11-to-1 return on investment, and more than $2 million in additional advocate-driven sales emanating just from the small, second group, Test Group B. Needless to say, the company is now fully rolling out this new strategy.

Travel industry leaders have always recognised the value of referrals in generating new business but until recently there haven't been any known systemic ways to boost referrals. By strategically providing customers with real tools that both encourage and train them to act as advocates, however, travel marketers can be assured they will quantifiably increase customer advocacy, and dramatically. Customers who feel confident speaking more knowledgeably (and thus eloquently) about a travel experience will be more inclined to do so. This means the prospective customer, the one being advocated to, will find his/her purchase decision has been made easier as well.

Upon learning about a given resort or cruise or hotel from a trusted source, including positive, informed features and benefits, the prospect moves more quickly along the customer-conversion cycle, becoming first a new customer and later an excited advocate. When offered the right tools, our new customer advocate becomes a knowledgeable advocate as well, passing on information as well as excitement to many others and generating referrals beneficial to all.

8

Human Resource in Hospitality Industry

Human resources (HR) as an important feature of long-term planning and nearly three-quarters felt their human resource practices, policies and procedures were aligned with their overall business strategy. As to the impact of technology, opinion was evenly split as to whether it will reduce the number of general staff required in the future, although there were some important differences regionally. In Asia / Pacific, close to two-thirds felt that technology would have this impact.

The role of HR management is not always clear in today's hospitality companies. Clearly the human resource function of the future will have a more bottom-line business orientation than it has had in the past. For this transition to be effective, however, a greater alignment of human capital management with the core business strategy will be required, coupled with more sophisticated measurements of performance. While the human resource function gets redefined within the organisation, its component parts are on offer without.

Increasingly popular as a tool for more effective business management, outsourcing appears destined to make in-roads into the HR function, part of a larger trend toward increased use of specialised vendors and other partners. In the future, we can expect to see more HR functions outsourced with one-third of respondents seeing training and benefits administration as outsource candidates for their organisations in the future.

Recruiting people to the hospitality industry is unfortunately only one of today's human capital challenges. Employee retention appears to be just as big a headache and it may get worse before it gets better. To counter this, approximately two-thirds of respondents plan an array of strategies, including the increased use of incentive pay, more job enrichment programmes, improved working conditions, improved screening tools and increases in benefits.

Once recruited, a number of strategies are used to reduce employee turnover—some effective, others less so. Improving the work environment, sharing information and increasing employee involvement in decision making are some of the leading choices. This suggests, however, that the hospitality industry may continue to find itself at a disadvantage when competing for qualified employees with better-paying industries. In looking at what contributes the most to employee turnover, there does not appear to be an overwhelmingly strong view in favor of any one factor. In order of significance, they were compensation, hours of work, opportunity for employment in other industries, benefits, work conditions, internal opportunity for growth and finally the image of the industry itself.

The relevance of hospitality education is an important issue for the industry as technology, finance and marketing become big drivers for success. Customer service as a vital educational issue—clearly a wellplaced priority that positions the customer at the center of the universe. An impressive majority of respondents also identified marketing as an important educational focus - a reflection of the growing competitiveness of the industry and of its increasing orientation to the customer.

TRAINING AND DEVELOPMENT OF EMPLOYEES

As hospitality organisations plan for the training and development of their employees in the future, they will evidently need to work more on their planning process—the current view is fairly negative. While just over two-thirds of respondents agreed that their training plan was 'effective', only 18 percent could "strongly agree" with such a statement. And one-third of respondents either took no position or viewed their plan as ineffective responses which suggest plenty of room for improvement.

As to training methods—"on the job" appears to be the dominant theme, although this approach should diminish somewhat in the future. Some of the more popular development programmes include multi-skilling, cross-training and career succession - and there are clear plans to significantly expand their use in the future. There also appears to be widespread use of employee participation programmes—close to two-thirds of respondents cite the use of suggestion schemes—a fairly traditional approach, while a surprisingly high 46 percent indicate job enrichment programmes and 43 percent so-called "quality circles".

Hospitality organisations also use a variety of methods to identify workplace issues and for the most part intend to significantly increase their use in the future. In US, employee surveys, currently used by 70 percent of respondents, are planned for an increase in the future. And while 68 percent of respondents acknowledge the use of suggestion boxes—the "employee" equivalent of the guest comment card—use of these passive instruments is expected to decline in the future.

As human capital becomes more expensive to recruit, train and develop, increasing attention is being devoted to those factors that affect productivity. Empowerment, education, training, recognition programmes and technology will all play different roles in this area in the future. The area with greatest prospective impact on productivity appears not surprisingly, to be training. Three out of four respondents held that empowerment, education, career advancement, incentive and recognition programmes would also have strong impacts on productivity in the future. Somewhat less impactful, was the role of technology.

Employee and Customer Satisfaction

In view of the evident relationship between employee and customer satisfaction, to rank the different approaches to improving the former. Employee recognition programmes, the opportunity for career advancement and exposure to training followed in order of impact. Improving performance is desirable but it also needs to be measured. In developing an integrated measurement system, the first step is to develop an accurate accounting of employee satisfaction. And to this end, a variety of methods are reportedly used. Employee surveys are destined for much greater usage in the future. And finally, upward evaluations now used by 18 percent are expected to more than double in use in the future.

Hospitality organisations around the globe appear to have set their priorities and will hopefully pursue these with the same vigor that they have historically applied in other areas of this complex capital and people intensive business. And for those that do, they will be in a far better position to compete in a world market space where human relationships and information will be valued far more highly than the physical assets that have been so central a part of the industry's makeup and psyche in the past.

Policy Dimensions of Human Resource Management

A "people" focus, within tourism and hospitality, is by no means new and successful organisations such as Disney, British Airways, Singapore Airlines, Marriott and Ritz Carlton have developed strong reputations for their recognition of the role which their staff play in meeting customer expectations within their sector. Best practice, in the area, appears to recognise that quality service delivery is not the outcome of an isolated service enhancement training programme, but has to do with change in organisational culture from top down and is a complex process which impacts on all areas of the organisation and its systems. It is also a process which is rather more commonly taken aboard within the context of larger organisations.

Small to medium-sized enterprises (SMEs), which have the advantage of simple internal communication systems, face other challenges reflective of their resource structures, expertise and nature of their workforce. There is little doubt that consumer experience of "human value added" through service is varied within and between the hospitality sectors of most countries. In part, this is a reflection of the eclectic nature of customer expectations which may demand very different things from the same service delivery situation. It is also a factor of the number of human interactions (moments of truth) which most customers experience within any one hospitality purchase—these may or may not be within the one organisation and thus the ability to "control" the customer's experience may not lie within the organisation, which suffers through lost business. In many respects, a customer's assessment of hospitality will be based on the total destination experience.

Human resource management is more than a strategic and operational concern for companies competing within the hospitality marketplace. It considers human resource management as a strategic dimension within the wider enhancement of quality and market positioning of tourism at the level of organisations, specific destinations, regions within countries or whole nations. The main thesis advanced is that the tourism and hospitality industry, from the perspective of all its stakeholders (public sector, private sector, visitors and host community), benefits from the close integration of human resource, labour market and education policies, with those policies relating to, and impacting on, the tourism and hospitality sector.

Human Resource in Hospitality Environment

The tourism and hospitality sector, in all locations, has a close relationship with the labour market environment from which it draws its skills and consequently depends on its workforce for the delivery of service and product standards to meet existing and anticipated demand from its visitor marketplace. This relationship is, on the one hand, one of dependency in that the make-up of the local workforce (or that which can be introduced into the local environment) has a direct influence on the standards and character of the tourist offering which can be prepared and presented to visitors—if local art and craft skills are not developed within the education system or at community level, it will not be possible to offer this dimension to visitors. On the other hand, tourism and hospitality, for many communities, provides a major and growing sector of the economy and, with it, employment opportunities which other traditional and declining sectors of the economy may not provide.

This is true in an industrial, urban context where cities such as Glasgow (now the second most visited urban centre in the UK) have developed tourism in the wake of the decline of its traditional heavy industrial sector. It is an equally valid scenario in locations where the exploitation of natural resources no longer provides the same level of employment opportunity as it did in the past—the decline of the North Atlantic fishery has seen island locations, such as the Faroes, Iceland, Greenland and Newfoundland, focus on tourism as part of wider economic diversification strategies.

Here illustrates, the two-way relationship between tourism and hospitality, and human resource development and management is not always recognised in a holistic and policy-focused manner by public or private sector concerns. Issues which literature and practical experience identified as the major human resource concerns faced by tourism and hospitality at both a practical, operational level and in the context of wider strategic and policy-oriented discussion. These were:

Demography and the shrinking employment pool resulting in labour and specific skills shortages. This is primarily a developed country phenomenon found in Western Europe, North America and "tiger economy" countries of the Far East. However, labour shortage is also a concern elsewhere when it is recognised that the specific skills which tourism demands (technical, cultural, communications) may be in short supply within many, less developed destination areas. Demographic and other forms of structural change within the labour market demand responses which take tourism recruitment beyond its traditional youth pool into consideration of mature worker alternatives (those returning to work; seeking a career change; retirees) and this, in turn, has major implications for relative remuneration, working conditions, employment security and related issues.

For many sub-sectors in tourism and hospitality, and in most developed countries, the negative employment image of the sector is a major issue and barrier to the recruitment and retention of quality and well educated employees. Both industry employees and wider society view hotel and catering labour as relatively low status, mainly because of the personal service nature of the work involved.

This poor image is the result of a cocktail of historic and contemporary factors—the origin of hospitality work within domestic service and its consequent associations with servility; links, in some countries, between hospitality employment and colonial legacy; widespread use of expatriate labour in many developing countries, creating the perception that the sector is one offering only limited opportunity for promotion and progression; widespread exposure to work in the sector as a first working experience, resulting in generalised assessment based on limited exposure; and the reality of anti-social working conditions and casualised remuneration.

In some respects, the negatively-held perceptions are not wholly justified by the reality of work for major airlines, international hotel groups, theme parks or within heritage organisations. In other regards, the perceptions are a mirror of the reality of work within an industrial sector dominated by small and medium-sized enterprises (SMEs) and the impact of irregular demand. The effect of these perceptions is to impose a barrier to employment and employment choice among school and college leavers, parents and career guidance teachers which has been very difficult to counter.

However, the situation, in some developing countries, is rather different in that international tourism offers a high status and secure employment environment when compared to alternatives in both the primary and manufacturing sectors. In some contexts, cultural and traditional perceptions may also militate against the recruitment of the best able and qualified recruits into the tourism and hospitality sector. Religious barriers, for example, may exclude some groups from participation, notably women.

As already indicated, the rewards and benefits structure of the tourism and hospitality industries can act as a barrier to the recruitment and retention of quality employees. This is a concern of particular focus within hospitality but perceptions regarding working conditions, hours and pay extend more generally across the tourism-related service sector. There is a clear and unavoidable reality, within tourism and hospitality, that the demand cycle is anti-social and falls out with "normal" nine-to-five working parameters. Aircraft fly at night, hotel guests expect services at weekends and theme parks reach peak demand during public holidays.

In terms of remuneration, the sector faces challenges in common with other labour-intensive service areas and in many countries has seen pressures for increased productivity alongside deskilling in many areas of work. At a policy level, the sector is influenced greatly by legislative intervention, for example European initiatives with respect to minimum wage levels, duration of the working week and unsociable working times.

Notwithstanding national and sub-sectoral diversity within tourism and hospitality, a combination of reality and perceptions gives an overall negative gloss to the image of many areas of the industry. This acts as a major barrier to the recruitment of quality personnel into work in the area. Many entrants to work in the sector do so with expectations of impermanence—this reflects reality in terms of the demand cycle (seasonality and fluctuations as a result of instability within the business cycle in general) whereby longer-term and sustained opportunities are not available to those who take employment in hotels, as resort couriers or ski instructors.

It is also reflective of short-termism within many tourism and hospitality businesses which may be unwilling to seek long-term commitment in return for reciprocal long-term investment in the recruit. The sector is one of unconstrained access to most of its working positions and one which, therefore, benefits from unrestrained recruitment to most of its positions but, conversely, also suffers because the skills it engenders in its workforce are in considerable demand within other areas of the service economy.

Thus, while entry is open, so is the opportunity to move out elsewhere, both within tourism and hospitality, and to other employment areas. Staff turnover, therefore, can be very high, especially in tight and competitive labour markets, and is a major inhibitor for organisations and destinations seeking to achieve overall enhancement of service and product quality.

A key issue, relating to recruitment, is that of specific skills shortages in key technical and some managerial areas. In part, this is an extension of the concerns addressed above—image, conditions, remuneration—but is also linked to a reluctance, within some industry sectors and businesses, to invest in the skills development of their key personnel. The Irish tourism industry, throughout a period of sustained growth from the mid-1980s onwards, has experienced acute shortages of key technical personnel, particularly chefs, despite levels of national unemployment considerably above the European Union average.

Contrary trends, however, also raise important issues with respect to recruitment and retention. The combined impact of technology and product substitution in the workplace; centralisation of key management functions (finance, information analysis, marketing); standardisation of product and service delivery; and delayering of management structures in many developed tourism economies means that opportunities for meaningful and developmental careers in skilled craft or managerial areas have been reduced. Reduced opportunity, in turn, impacts on perceptions of the sector and the likelihood of young people, in particular, opting for tourism/hospitality as their career choice.

A changing tourism and hospitality industry environment is, in a sense, complemented but also complicated by changing social expectations of work and an increasingly diverse profile of employees. Diversity provides the opportunity to create new working environments and conditions, but demands comprehensive review of traditional practice. A good example of this is the present reluctance of many employees to accept split-shift working and the consequent need for employers to reorganise their work environment accordingly.

Education, training and development, for tourism and hospitality is also, in part, a recruitment issue in that providers of educational and training programmes, particularly within the college and university sector, are influenced by the same perceptual factors as the industry itself. Recruitment standards to vocational programmes for the sector are lower than those to equivalent courses in related professional areas, for example business. Tourism studies are, in a sense, somewhat different from hospitality in this respect in that vocational outcomes are less clearly defined and graduate choice is likely to be rather more eclectic.

There are clear opportunities to use such educational programmes in a rather more general education sense rather than facing clear vocational channelling. One key issue is a lack of tourism sector consensus as to the need for sector-specific educational provision. Commitment to ongoing career development of existing employees, within tourism and hospitality, varies greatly and is influenced by the sub-sector and the size of the enterprise. The presence of career development opportunities, however, is likely to exert a considerable influence on the retention of ambitious employees, with potential, within the sector.

Recognition remains relatively limited that human resource development is an important contributor to the delivery of quality products and service, within tourism and hospitality, and that this, in turn, impacts on the level of both new and repeat business achieved by businesses and destinations. This situation has altered significantly in recent years and the business advantage achieved, through a people focus, by companies such as British Airways, Singapore Airlines, Marriott and Ritz Carlton, has been an important contributory factor.

However, many small businesses do not have the resources or skills to focus on their human capital. Given that tourism destinations have images that are only as strong as their weakest link, it is important to strive to ensure that the visitor's experience is positive throughout the full range of contact with the providers of goods and services. Human resource development is, frequently, addressed as a reactive concern within tourism and hospitality, and rarely in a proactive and planned sense.

Product and market shifts and developments may be the target of strategic analysis and preparation, but it is not common, within the sector, to find enterprises or wider destination communities putting in place recruitment, education and training in support of such change, whether quantitative or qualitative in advance. Recognition of the lead-time needed to achieve benefit from human resource investment is also limited at both corporate and national levels.

Skills in the Hospitality Industry

In the context of hospitality, skills issue is informed by wider, generic debate about changing employment and vocational education within both developed and developing economies. Hospitality work exhibits diversity in both horizontal and vertical terms. In a horizontal sense, it includes a very wide range of jobs, the extent depending upon the definition of the sector that is employed. The traditional research focus on hospitality work concentrates on areas that provide, primarily, food and beverage and, to a lesser extent, accommodation.

Research into wider areas of hospitality work, particularly those that have emerged with the expansion of services and functions in the area (front desk, leisure, entertainment, reservations call centres) is much more poorly served and draws on a limited range of work in these areas. The 'newer' areas include functions and tasks that exhibit considerable crossover with work that falls outside normal definitions of hospitality in food and drink manufacture, office administration, IT systems management and specialist areas of sports and leisure.

Indeed, it is fair to say that although there is long-standing debate as to whether the hospitality industry is 'unique', there is little doubt that there is little that is unique about hospitality skills. Most of the skills that are employed within the sector also have relevance and application in other sectors of the service economy. Those employed in areas where there is considerable skills overlap with hospitality may well see themselves in terms of their generic skills area rather than as part of the hospitality labour market and some of these skills have been subject to separate assessment in a manner that has value and crossover implications for the hospitality sector.

The characteristics and the organisation of the hospitality industry are subject to on-going re-structuring and evolutionary change. There are major labour market and skills implications of such change as businesses re-shape the range of services they offer or respond to fashion and trend imperatives in the consumer marketplace. Vertical diversity in hospitality work is represented by a more traditional classification that ranges from unskilled through semi-skilled and skilled to supervisory and management. This 'traditional' perspective of work and, therefore, skills in hospitality is partly described by Riley, in terms that suggest that the proportionate breakdown of the workforce in hospitality is as follows:

Managerial - 6%

Supervisory - 8%

Craft (skilled) - 22%

Operative (semi-skilled and unskilled) - 64%

This simplification masks major business organisational diversity in hospitality, reflecting the size, location and ownership of hospitality businesses. The actual job and skills content of work in hospitality is predicated upon these factors so that common job titles (for example, restaurant manager, sous chef) almost certainly mask a very different range of responsibilities, tasks and skills within jobs in different establishments.

Riley is useful in his application of the weak-strong internal labour market model to illustrate the relationship that his workforce structure has to a number of externalities including educational requirements, points of entry into the workforce, workplace pay differentials and level of trade union membership. This analysis has important ramifications for the status of hospitality work and the perceived attractiveness of the sector both for employment and educational/training opportunity. Some of the researchers summarise a list of the characteristics of hospitality work that tend to confirm Riley's weak internal labour market attribution:

— Tendency to low wages, except where skills shortages act to counter this.

— Prevalence of unsocial hours and family unfriendly shift patterns.

— Rare incidence of equal opportunities policies and male domination of higher level, better paid work.

— Poor or non-existent career structures.

— Informal recruitment practices.

— Failure to adopt formalised 'good' or 'best' practice models of human resource management and development.

— Lack of any significant trade union presence.

— High levels of labour turnover.

— Difficulties in recruitment and retention.

The skills profile of hospitality, in turn, is influenced by the labour market that is available to it, both in direct terms and via educational and training establishments. The weak internal labour market characteristics in themselves impose downward pressures on the skills expectations that employers have of their staff and this, in turn, influences the nature and level of training which the educational system delivers. There is an evident cycle of down-skilling, not so much in response to the actual demands of hospitality work or of consumer expectations of what it can deliver, but as a result of the perceptions of potential employees and the expectations that employers have of them.

Hospitality work is widely characterised in both the popular press and in research-based academic sources as dominated by a low skills profile or, as brutally and, probably, unfairly put it, 'uneducated, unmotivated, untrained, unskilled and unproductive.' However, Burns questions the basis for categorising hospitality employment into 'skilled' and 'unskilled' categories, arguing the postmodernist case that this separation is something of a social construct that is rooted in, firstly, manpower planning paradigms for the manufacturing sector and, secondly, in the traditional power of trade unions to control entry into the workplace through lengthy apprenticeships.

Burns bases this argument on a useful consideration of the definition of skills in hospitality, noting that: ...the different sectors that comprise tourism-as-industry take different approaches to their human resources, and that some of these differences...are due to whether or not the employees have a history of being 'organised' (either in terms of trade unions or staff associations with formalised communication procedures).

This strong internal labour market analysis leads Burns to argue that skills within 'organised' sectors such as airlines and hotel companies with clearly defined staff relationship structures are recognised and valued. By contrast, catering and fast food 'operate within a business culture where labour is seen in terms of costs which must be kept at the lowest possible level' and where skills, therefore, are not valued or developed. Burns' definition of hospitality skills also seeks to go beyond the purely technical capabilities that those using 'unskilled' or 'low skills' descriptors assume.

He draws upon the oft used dramaturgical analogy for the service workplace to argue that 'Working in such an environment requires more than an ability to operate a cash register; emotional demands are made of employees to constantly be in a positive, joyful and even playful mood. An ability to cope with such demands must be recognised as a "skill" par excellence.' New employees in hospitality 'Must be trained to be loyal, flexible, tolerant, amiable and responsible...at every successful tourism establishment, it is the employees that stand out...Technology cannot substitute for welcoming employees.'

Burns' emphasis on 'emotional demands' as an additional dimension of hospitality skills. Work in both fast food and traditional areas of service work areas demands considerable emotional elements in addition to any overt technical skills. Furthermore, Burns rightly argues that the low skills perspective of hospitality is contextspecific and is drawn from a western-centric view of hospitality work and skills generally. He cites the inappropriateness of these assumptions when applied to environments such as the Solomon Islands, Sri Lanka and the Cook Islands.

In the developing world, such assumptions cannot be made as employees join hospitality businesses without western acculturation, without knowledge of the implements and ingredients of western cookery, for example. Learning at a technical level, therefore, is considerably more demanding than it might be in western communities. Social and inter-personal skills also demand considerably more by way of prior learning, whether this pertains to language skills or wider cultural communications.

The current hospitality labour market in the Republic of Ireland illustrates this situation where service standards are under challenge as the industry recruits staff from a wide range of former eastern block countries. A government-sponsored response has been to organise special training programmes of three months duration for new workers from Poland and Russia. The low skills argument also tends to neglect the opportunities that hospitality provides for the relatively easy access to the use of entrepreneurial and management skills.

Weak internal labour market characteristics mean that it is readily feasible for those with limited specific hospitality or business training to enter the industry at ownership or senior management levels, especially in the independent sector. The aim of many who enter the sector is to eventually start up their own business. Others may choose to do so after careers in different areas of

In reality, such work represents multi-tasking because the level and nature of the work in question (food service, bar service, portering, housekeeping) offers little by way of enhancing the actual skills of employees other than extending the operational context within which they are exercised. One of the specialist educational programme represents the accumulation of complementary but not progressive skills in various hotel departments.

The issue of multi-skilling or multi-tasking should be seen in the context of organisational change within hospitality and the manner in which organisations are separating core employees in whom significant training and skills development is invested and those at the periphery for whom such enhancement is not common. It is argued that developing skills across a range of functional areas enhances the likelihood of acceptance within the core although evidence for this is not readily available. Creating the opportunity to develop a wider range of skills within the workplace is frequently included within models of job enrichment.

Multi-skilling or multi-tasking across departments, as generally practiced within the hospitality sector, does not offer much to employees that can be described as 'enriching'. Of probably greater value to employees is the breakdown of job demarcation within hospitality departments, such as the virtual elimination of the traditional partie system within kitchens and the merging of front office functions (cashier, reception, concierge) in many hotels.

Generic Skills

Skills shortages in hospitality are increasingly seen in terms of generic rather than specific technical competencies. Studies of employer expectations of graduates note demand for communications, people management and problem solving. It is, of course, an issue that informs a debate across the service sector - see for example, Tesco as well as within the wider economy with their development of core or key skills. Qualifications and Curriculum Authority (QCA) identifies key skills as:

— Communications.
— Application of number.
— Information Technology.
— Working with others.
— Improving own learning and performance.

These key skills represent capabilities that have, traditionally, been integrated as 'normal' expectations within hospitality curricula at operational and management levels and a specific focus on the development of these skills, outside main curriculum delivery objectives, may be questionable in the context of this sector.

However, Hospitality Training Foundation (HtF) continue to report employer demands for improved generic skills as a priority. These skills include communications, showing initiative, delivering customer service and demonstrating a willingness to learn. Recommendations to tackle the generic skills gap include:

— Building generic skills development into full-time education programmes.
— Funding for training providers to deliver key skills and develop appropriate aptitudes and attitudes within young people.
— Ensuring providers are developed to be able to deliver key skills.
— Recruitment practices need to encompass generic skills requirements.

HtF's Delphi study of skills requirements in hospitality also reports that the skills gaps, as seen by the hospitality industry, focus on what can be styled the generic agenda - communications, problem solving and customer service in addition to job specific skills.

Empirical evidence from a study of front office work and skills requirements across a number of European countries shows clearly that this focus operates in practice. Hotels in all quality categories in seven European countries recruit on the basis of generic employability rather than specific skills and experience. Even five star hotels 'accept the reality of the marketplace and are willing to recruit staff without Front Office experience provided they have good general education and a willingness to learn.' The same report also notes that: A key evolving change in Front Office work is the integration of technical and interpersonal skills in all aspects of work. This is the result of a growing emphasis on the latter while technology has developed as a support for the delivery of service rather than as an objective in itself. In a technical sense, technology will continue to reduce the skills demands of Front Office work as systems become more user friendly and share their basic operating features with widely used office and domestic computer software.

The weakening of traditional workplace hierarchies in front office, with a decline in the position of junior or assistant receptionist so that given 'the virtual elimination of traditional, routine office-related tasks such as basic typing, filing and photocopying, it is, in any case, difficult to distinguish between the job content' of various levels of work within the area. In the absence of experienced, qualified staff, many hotels will increasingly look to generic, non-technical competencies (communication, problem solving, customer service and IT) in recruiting new personnel and build in extended on-the-job-training within the induction phase'.

In addition to these generic skills considerations, some of the studies suggests that aesthetic criteria also feature increasingly prominently in the recruitment of front line staff for hospitality work. HtF's skills and employment forecasts raise an interesting paradox in the hospitality skills debate. Employers, as has been demonstrated, place value on generic skills such as the willingness to learn and the ability to be flexible and adaptive. At the same time, initiative is also a valued skill and one found to be lacking in the industry. HtF raise two important questions:

— Are employers being unrealistic in their expectations? People who are good at following instructions may not be able to show much initiative.

— Are employers recruiting the 'right' people? If, when recruiting, employers focus on people they feel are good at following instructions, they may find later that they cannot expect them to show much initiative.

These questions are of particular relevance in the context of trends towards and advocacy for greater empowerment in learning and work. The concept of empowerment is presented in the hospitality management literature as a human resource strategy with relatively widespread application.

TRAINING IN HOSPITALITY INDUSTRY

Travel and tourism represents a broad range of related industries. The growth of these industries has opened up many new job opportunities for graduates in areas such as:

— hotels

— restaurants

— retailing

— transportation

— travel agencies
— tour companies
— tourist attractions
— leisure, recreation and sport
— cultural industries

It is interesting to realise that in 1997 travel and tourism provides 10.5% of the total world employment, with up to 25% of all employment, in some areas, such as the Caribbean. It has been estimated that, by 2007, more than 100 million people world-wide will be employed in this sector. Because of this, tourism is now seen to be of importance to most countries of the world.

During this time, the nature of tourism has developed in scope and direction, away from traditional activities, such as the sunshine sand and sea holidays to a wide range of new activities such as cultural tourism, adventure tourism, sports and leisure activities and eco-tourism.

Given the potential for interesting and rewarding careers in these industries many young people are looking for suitable courses which will help prepare them for careers in management within the tourism and hospitality industries. When looking at courses in hospitality and tourism, there can seem to be a bewildering variety of course titles covering the main employment areas of travel, tourism, hotels and restaurants.

The hospitality industry is now considering putting much effort on education, and of the element to be paid attention is training and development. Rapid changing in environment must be dealt with 'freedom' of creativity, new approaches to staff, dealing with new technology conveying learning into their life at work, flexibility in organisation model, etc have become part of daily activities. All these issues are really now the driving forces for the hospitality industry to 'tap in' into the current environment. The question is how the whole 'perplexing' issues can be answered in today's business life.

The hospitality industry ought to rely on model of strategic business management to accelerate the sensitivity of growing expectations from customers. The model below attempts to accommodate the variety of issues in today's environment as part of the strategic model. The hospitality industry must realise that designing a model of the strategic management ought to be looking at the wide range of components that might be affecting its performance.

One of the main thing should be addressed is the dynamic environment. All aspects of factors beyond the industry have put in place before proceeding to the plan. Identifying the variety of environment can be valuable for both the company and its clients. No longer 'gambling' or 'intuitive' or 'personal feelings' recommendation to establish the business objectives. One thing should be done is compiling significant information of existing market and trying to break them down into scale of priorities.

One of the difficulties facing the hospitality industry these days is hiring the skilled person(s) to synthesise relevant information. The critical point here is the hospitality industry must be able to accommodate its current resources and be persistent about where we want to go. A lot of experts argue that a strategic management model can only be applied to anticipate the changing environment.

Unfortunately, this is not right. What managers should do is developing the model and 'engineering' the environment to fit with the proposed model. One possible method is to create a market that attracts customers to come, and ensure they will come back again. Price and quality could have been used as the tools to create new opportunities. The model above might be used to put some ideas to fix the old paradigm of 'anticipating' and 'adjusting' model and move to a 'dynamic' model that can be flexible in current and future environment.

By (always) related back to your vision and strategic objectives, the hospitality industry has to catch up with future environment. The problem within the hospitality industry is having a lack of vision, and the industry has only long-term strategic plans. What happens with the environment is it changes rapidly. Therefore, the hospitality industry must make and develop its strategic model to speed up its role of current and future environment. This means that the hospitality industry ought to focus primarily upon the needs of all employees be reoriented to changing conditions.

The human aspects should be given more attention in today's environment. The model above depicted that understanding and underlying the importance of the strategic business objectives in line with corporate vision should be transformed into 'transferable manner' that employees might able to follow them up. Thus, it certainly requires management's support (i. e. motivation, reinforcement, reward and recognition). The central focus on this model is the hospitality industry must come up with strategies to achieve goals.

One possible strategy is to provide training and development that will lead to learning. Encouraging learning has become one of an international theme within the hospitality industry. There have been a lot of discussions in this matter whether an organisation should provide a specific training for a specific job or we offer a training package leading to multiskilling employees. This is "an old song in the new rhythms".

The issue is not just be able to improve skills, but mastered in specific skills instead. The main concern in the hospitality industry that customers demand professionalism on the jobs. If you are able to have different skills for different jobs, that's excellent. But, don't get too excited not being able to provide an outstanding service. The principle for the training process therefore getting new personnel and current staff to be able to play a role to the success of the organisation and then how the services or products of the organisation can contribute to society.

The model indicates that the first step to be taken is induction programmes that are familiarising new employees to the organisation, their job, and the work unit. During induction programmes, the hospitality industry tend to explain in details about the philosophy, culture, ways doing things, etc. This is quite right in one side to ensure that new employees are able to identify their current internal environment. However, this could be downgrading employees' expectation that may have different approaches about the existing atmosphere.

Instead of giving employees a bulk of big manuals to them, it would be better off for employees to adapt and be motivated that your contribution is really significant for our goals. One way to attain this is through socialisation that encourages employees to unite with current employees. Socialisation is the process through which new employees acquire the knowledge, skills, and attitudes that make them successful and to be integrated to the organisation and work department. Be ensure that the training programmes can and must encourage participants to learn, and managers have to motivate them to ensure that they will apply the new acquired skills in the worksite and learning transfer should be prioritised among managers. Conducting evaluation would be the possible tool to find out whether training has been transferred or not is.

Evaluation may be the least area to be considered and developed. Having 'smile sheets' is insufficient to render judgment about the effectiveness of your training activities, but it must involve the whole components (i. e. trainees' reaction, learning issues, behaviour and results) to find out how effective the programmes are. When the evaluation is completed, we are able to expect that the outcomes are positive and rewarding, both for those responsible for the programmes and for managers who will make decisions derived from their evaluation training programmes.

The basic issue in the hospitality industry that a certain model must be developed to endeavor to lead in the future market. The hospitality industry a picture of how necessary every step should be considered to execute the training programmes. Working on wrong assumptions may lead to design inappropriate training programmes that could create 'an undesired outcomes'. The current issues occurred in the workforce and attempt to 'tap in' into the model.

The model into the current issues is the hospitality industry will be in favor position to compete in a world environment that in line with companies' vision and strategic objectives by designing the appropriate training programmes. More importantly, human relationships, information and willing to change will be seen as very imperative to attain desired outcomes. The model chosen attempts to accommodate the topical themes in the hospitality industry.

Training in Serving Customers

Training is about skills, knowledge and attitudes. Training is nothing more than providing you with the basic ability to provide uniformly high standards of service (how). An individual can demonstrate his or her ability (skills) to perform, then this individual does not require any more training. If someone possesses 'an adequate' skill, thus training is necessary to perform tasks 'according to standards'.

To explore here is 'something' beyond the training programmes for persons who have had enough experience in the field. This may have been hidden for quiet long time. Again, in the hospitality industry, managers tend to seek someone who has a basic skill to perform (how well), and then from that basis, a new employee will be assigned to undertake further training to 'polish' with work standards (how). Thus, it appears that your past experience is 'only' working during recruitment and selection process.

Training programme is provided in line with the work standards. Most of the training managers have their own agenda to supply the industry with 'qualified staff' and this has to be done to achieve companies' vision and strategic objectives. However, there is one missing point here that the training programmes offered may far than staff's expectations. Experienced staff does not want any 'basic' skills anymore, but using his or her past experience to jump up to the next level, therefore, they require management development programmes. Managers may argue that we 'expect' you to serve our guests according to the manuals and should follow literally.

Everything has run smoothly and beautifully and there were not any mistakes. At the end of the day, managers will evaluate and give you a positive feedback. However, it was not the way it works at this hotel. The hotel expects you differently. It is only a matter of the 'right way' to service guests. The word 'expect' will sound explicitly. It can be seen that what happens to staff depends not just upon "how well" you serve, but also upon "how" you serve customers. "How well" you serve is related to individuals' skills, whereas "how" you serve customers is a matter of work procedures.

Having had work experience is the good one and this may be useful to support your career progress. But, once again, if you have failed to execute the hotel work standards, it seemed unlikely for every staff to be promoted. Originally, training programmes in the hospitality industry purpose:

— to support staff with basic skills required to perform tasks,
— to provide additional training (if it is required) to reduce the performance discrepancies, or to support for a new position,
— to supply employees to be able to carry the company's banner,
— to provide for staff with new acquired knowledge to achieve customers' expectation,
— to offer staff with 'appropriate' attitudes, and certain knowledge,
— lastly, managers expect staff to work uniformly high standards

Taylored Training Targets

The "core competencies" cover the skills necessary for the continued personal and organisational success in the hospitality industry, including customer service, writing, and meetings skills. To provide the training necessary to put these skills in place. The "managerial competencies" address the leadership and practical skills needed to cultivate an effective and productive managerial force, including sales, leadership and career management.

Communication and team-building are the focus of the "strategic competencies" segment, and thc "tactical competencies" cover sales and marketing. Among the current programmes, which can be presented at in-house, off-site, or at regional locations, are:

— Creating a Culture of Customer Service

— ServSafe Food Safety Certification

— Marketing For The Hotel Industry: Understanding The Individual Leisure And Corporate Customer

— Presentation Skills: Staying Calm And Confident Before Two or 2000!

— It's Not Rocket Science!—Boot Camp for New Sales People

— Building A Web Site That Works

Taylored Training's primary resource is a panel of presenters and trainers with extensive and specialised professional experience, giving them unique understanding and insight into all facets of the hospitality industry. Panel expertise may also be drawn upon for conferences, education sessions, meetings and private consultations.

9

Careers in Hospitality Industry

Hospitality Management, including the Food Service Industry, is one of the fastest growing occupations in the world. There are predictions that by the year 2005 there will be 12 million workers in this industry. Food Service personnel are needed at the rate of one to every 10 to 12 positions, and the industry is seeking those with a culinary and hospitality education to meet the complex demands of the 21st century. How will you know if you would be good in these careers? The hospitality industry is comprised of friendly, courteous, and helpful individuals who are willing to deliver great customer service with a passion. If you possess these qualities and have good communication skills, then this exciting industry could be for you.

Upon graduation, students of Hospitality Management and Culinary Arts schools may seek employment in hotels, restaurants, catering, resorts, cruise ships, casinos, and entertainment venues, just to mention a few. Jobs in hospitality operations can be found in almost every community in the United States and abroad. Earning potential varies and is limited only by your ability and willingness to succeed. Starting wages are $8 to $16 per hour; however, this can increase substantially with experience and perseverance. Many Hospitality Management positions offer benefits such as health insurance, paid vacations and sick days, and reduced rates on accommodations, food, and travel. Annually, travel and tourism employers around the world pay more than $1.6 trillion in wages and salaries and create 12.5 million new jobs.

Hospitality is an industry that is known for promoting from within and for having a large number of young managers. If you're talented and demonstrate a good work ethic, you can advance quickly. There is no limit to where your dreams and ambitions can take you in the exciting and fascinating world of Hospitality Management. Remember, it is not where you start that matters, it's where you finish. It is important for you to select an industry segment appropriate to your ability and personality.

Skills Inventory

One of the best ways to select a career niche you will be happy with is to start by listing your own skills. What are the tasks you do best? Most skills fall into one of three areas: skills dealing with data, skills dealing with people, or skills dealing with things. You will probably find that the majority of your skills will fall into one or two of these areas.

People whose skills fall into the data group are often good in subjects such as math and science and enjoy working with computers. They tend to like such activities as analysing information, comparing figures, working with graphs, and solving abstract problems. Such individuals might enjoy doing feasibility studies for a hospitality management consulting firm. They might also be happy in the corporate planning departments of large hotel and restaurant chains, where data is analysed and demand is forecast.

Most auditors and accountants fall into the data-skills group. If you like to deal with people, you probably enjoy helping them and taking care of their needs. You can take and give advice and instructions. You may also enjoy supervising and motivating other people, and may find that they respond to your leadership. Individuals with people skills are often good at negotiating and selling-they like to bargain and are not afraid to make decisions. In the hospitality industry, general managers and marketing and sales managers of hotels often fall into this category. So do independent restaurant owners, catering managers, and dub managers.

Hospitality Industry

Why do people go into the hospitality industry? If you were to ask people who have spent their careers in this business what they like most about it, you would get a wide variety of answers. Some of the most popular are:

— *The industry offers more career options than most.* No matter what kind of work you enjoy, and wherever your aptitudes lie, there is a segment of the industry that can use your talents (take another look at Exhibit I!).

— *The work is varied.* Because hotels and restaurants are complete production, distribution, and service units, managers are involved in a broad array of activities.

— *There are many opportunities to be creative.* Hotel and restaurant managers might design new products to meet the needs of their guests; produce training programmes for employees; or implement challenging advertising, sales promotion, and marketing plans.

— *This is a "people" business.* Managers and supervisors spend their workdays satisfying guests, motivating employees, and negotiating with vendors and others.

— *Hospitality jobs are not nine-to-five jobs.* Hours are highly flexible in many positions.

— *There are opportunities for long-term career growth.* If you are ambitious and energetic, you can start with an entry-level job and move up. The industry is full of stories of people who started as bellpersons or cooks and rose to high management positions or opened their own successful businesses.

— *There are perks associated with many hospitality jobs.* If you become- the general manager of a resort, you can dine at its restaurants with your family and friends, and use its recreational facilities. Airline and cruise employees get free or reduced-fare travel.

Despite these advantages, there are some aspects of the business that many people don't like:

— *Long hours.* In most hospitality businesses the hours are long. The 40-hour workweek is not the norm, and 50- to 60-hour workweeks are not unusual.

— *Nontraditional schedules.* Hospitality managers do not work a Monday through-Friday schedule. In the hospitality field you will probably often find yourself working when your friends are relaxing. As one manager told his employees, "If you can't come to work Saturday or Sunday, don't bother to come in on Monday."

— *Pressure.* There are busy periods when managers and employees are under intense pressure to perform.

— *Low beginning salaries.* Entry-level jobs for management trainees tend to be lowpaying compared to some other industries.

Travel Industry Jobs

Eating and drinking places are the leading source of travel industry jobs. This is due to the labour intensiveness of the industry and the high proportion of traveller dollars spent on food. During 1995, eating and drinking places employed 7.35 million workers. Approximately 25 percent of these jobs were directly attributable to travel and tourism. Eating and drinking places provide a variety of job opportunities, including, but not limited to:

Executive Chefs	District Managers
Accountants	Waiters
Unit Managers	Advertising Specialists
Food Preparation Workers	Hosts and Hostesses
General Managers	Controllers
Public Relations	Dieticians
Food Service	Managers Purchasing Agents
Bartenders	Personnel Directors

There is a great deal of diversity in eating and drinking establishments, including hundreds of thousands of small businesses and many large chain-owned restaurants.

The types of jobs available in smaller independent restaurants consist almost entirely of cooks, cashiers, and waiters/waitresses. Managers tend to be promoted from within by excelling in entry-level positions. Larger restaurants employ general managers as well as assistant managers. At the top of the restaurant spectrum are luxury restaurants, which are for the most part owned and operated by independent entrepreneurs. Within the trade, these restaurants are sometimes called "white tablecloth" restaurants. Most of their patrons are on expense accounts.

Chain-Restaurant

Chain restaurants recruit the majority of their managers from hospitality schools. Entry-level jobs for graduates with hospitality degrees are often on the assistant-manager level, with progression to manager, then district manager responsible for a group of restaurants, and then regional manager. Restaurant chains are the fastest growing part of the restaurant business today. Many of these chains are made up of fast-food restaurants or, as they prefer to be called, "quick-service" restaurants. Menus rarely change in these restaurants. Their strategy calls for delivering a large number of meals at fairly low prices. These firms, however, offer a variety of executive and management positions in the following career path:

Management Trainee
to
Assistant Manager
to
Unit Manager
to
District Manager
to
Regional Manager

Corporate headquarters of chain-restaurants offer the same type of top executive positions as other large firms across all industries. These include CEOs, COOs, CFOs, and several Vice President levels.

Social Caterers

Social catering is another part of the food service industry that many hospitality graduates become interested in. Catering is another business that is most often started by independent entrepreneurs, as it requires very little start-up capital-facilities can be rented as needed, equipment can usually be' leased on a short-term basis from restaurant supply houses, and food servers can be hired as needed. In some cases, caterers provide only food; in others, they are responsible for tables, chairs, utensils, tents, servers, and decorations.

Contract Food Companies

Contract food companies are generally hired by organisations whose major business purpose is not food service, but they provide it for some reason. The biggest users of contract food services are large manufacturing and industrial concerns in which workers have a short lunch period. Contractors such as ARAMARK and Sodexho operate cafeterias and executive dining rooms for these companies.

The service is often subsidised by the contracting company, which may supply the space and utilities and, in some cases, underwrite some or all of the food costs. Schools and colleges, hospitals, sports arenas, airlines, cruise ships, and even prisons use contract food companies. In the case of airlines, meals are cooked and prepackaged in central commissaries and then delivered to the airplanes for preparation and service as needed.

Contract food management is somewhat unusual because the manager must please two sets of employers-the manager's home office and the client that has contracted for the service. Many contract food programmes, such as those at schools and hospitals, have strong nutritional requirements as well. Others, such as airline programmes, require knowledge of advanced food technology.

Careers in contract food service are attractive to many hospitality majors. Contract food managers work more regular hours and are under less pressure than restaurant managers. Why? Because many of the users of contract food service, such as office building tenants, work a regular 40-hour week, Monday through Friday, which allows the contract food managers to work more normal hours. Also, contract food managers are able to predict with more certainty how many people they are going to feed, what they will feed them, and when the meals will be served. Because of the large volume of meals involved, contract food managers must be highly skilled in professional management techniques and cost control. For this reason, contract food companies usually hire people with experience within their industry and recruit from hospitality schools.

Institutional Food Service

Although contract food companies can supply food for schools and hospitals, the majority of these institutions handle their own food service programmes. Most public schools belong to the National School Lunch Programme established by the federal government in 1946. The purpose of this programme is twofold: (1) to create a market for agricultural products produced by America's farmers, and (2) to serve a nutritious lunch to schoolchildren at a low cost. Public elementary schools tend to offer only those menu items that qualify for government support, but many high schools add items such as hamburgers, French fries, and even diet sodas.

High school food managers work hard to come up with creative and innovative menu plans to keep students in school cafeterias. Even the look of school cafeterias has changed as managers have developed new methods of merchandising food.

Colleges and universities have also experienced changes in their food service programmes. Because more students live off-campus now, there is a trend toward flexible meal plans in which students have a choice of how many meals they wish to purchase from the institution. To compete successfully, many universities have opened special table-service restaurants in addition to their traditional cafeterias. Another move has been to offer a more varied cafeteria menu featuring salad bars and popular items such as croissant sandwiches, bagels, lox and cream cheese, and even Belgian waffles for breakfast. Some universities have brought on campus quick-service outlets such as Pizza Hut and Taco Bell.

Hospital programmes are usually administered by a trained dietitian or a professional food service manager working with one. Menus are generally simple and nourishing. In the past, most hospitals had a central kitchen where all foods were prepared and then sent in insulated carts or trays to the patients rooms. Some hospitals have decentralized their food service. With a decentralised system, the hospital purchases frozen and portionpacked entrees and salads and keeps them in small pantries in various parts of the hospital. The meals are then plated and heated in microwave ovens as needed. Another trend has been the attempt to turn hospital food service from a cost center into a revenue center. Some hospitals sell take-home food to doctors and employees and even do outside catering.

> Institutions are beginning to compete with commercial food service operations for consumers, This means that there are more opportunities than ever before for hospitality students to enter what is clearly a growing field.
>
> Executive employment within eating and drinking places, including top management, general managers, accountants, and auditors, numbered 427,000 in 1994. These top executive-level jobs are expected to grow by 30.8 percent by the year 2005. This compares with a much slower growth rate of 14.9 percent for total U.S. employment.
>
> According to the Department of Commerce, over half of all restaurants employ less than ten workers, significantly fewer than businesses in most other industries. This means that resta-urants offer a better chance than most industries for self ownership. According to the BLS, there are 276,000 workers in the industry who are self-employed or family workers in a family owned business. This is more employment than provided by the entire steel manufacturing industry in the U.S.

Employment in Air Transportation

Air transportation represents the largest employment sector of the transportation segment of the transportation segment of the travel and tourism industry. This sector comprised 748,000 jobs in 1994 and 787,000 employees in 1995. Employment in air transportation offers a wide variety of technical and managerial jobs. A brief list of the types of job opportunities available in air transportation includes:

Pilots	Baggage Handlers
Customer Service Representative	Aircraft Mechanics
Reservations and Ticket Agent	Flight Attendants
Public Relations	Food Service Workers
General Managers	Controllers
CEOs and other top executives	

Employment within the air transportation industry usually requires specialised skills and training. Jobs such as pilots and mechanics need to be certified by the Federal Aviation Administration. The advancement ladder for a pilot starts as flight engineer followed by co-pilot followed by captain. Advancement also exists by moving from small airlines to larger airlines.

Mechanics require a great deal of technical training and there are opportunities to advance to head mechanic or supervisory positions. Flight attendants need to have good personal interactive skills, as they must deal constantly with the travelling public. Although flight attendants are considered to be limited in advancement, opportunities do exist to become customer service directors, instructors, and recruiting representatives.

Like flight attendants, reservations clerks need to deal constantly with the public. Advancement tends to be limited to supervisory positions, although it is possible to advance to district sales managers and into marketing positions. Executive employment within the air transportation industry, including top management, general managers, and accountants and auditors, numbered 39,000 in 1994. These top-level executive jobs are expected to grow by 16.2 percent by the year 2005.

Other Employment Opportunities

Hotels, motels, and other lodging establishments employed over 1.6 million Americans in 1994 and slightly over 1.65 million in 1995. Nearly all this employment is directly generated by travel and tourism. A brief list of some of the employment opportunities offered within this industry includes:

Marketing Representatives	Housekeepers
Front Desk Clerks	General Managers
Chief Engineers	Reservation Clerks
Food and Beverage Directors	Bellman
Front Office Managers	Personnel Directors
Meeting/Conference Planner	Controllers
Concierges	CEOs and other top executives

The hotel industry, like the eating and drinking industry, has a great deal of diversity in the types of establishments and, therefore, the types of jobs offered. The smaller "mom and pop" hotels generally offer limited employment opportunities. However, it is important to keep in mind that these establishments are fulfilling small business ownership goals.

Larger hotels and chain hotel firms offer a large number and variety of job opportunities, as well as advancement potential. Headquarters of chainhotels, for example, offer the typical top executive positions such as CEOs, COOs, various department heads, and Vice President positions. In recent years, hotel operations have become more service-oriented and have required a great deal more job responsibility for guest contact employees. Demand for persons who have skills obtained in colleges, junior colleges, and technical institutes is increasing, as most uppermanagement positions require considerable training.

Career paths exist within many departments of large hotel properties. Supervisory positions exist in food and beverage operations, front office management, personnel, marketing and accounting department to name a few. Executive employment within the lodging industry, including top management, general managers, accountants and auditors, numbered 123,000 in 1994. These top executive level jobs are expected to grow by 27.8 percent by the year 2005.

Would you rather be part of a large chain or work for an independent operation? There are many opportunities in both areas. The arguments for working for a large chain include:

— *Better training*. Companies such as Ritz-Carlton and Hyatt have very sophisticated operating systems.

— *More Opportunities for advancement*. Hotel managers of chain properties who wish to advance might be offered opportunities for promotions within the division in which they work or, if none are available there, in different divisions

— *Better benefits*. You are more likely to get superior life and health insurance benefits, more generous vacation and sick time, use of a company car, moving expenses, stock purchase options, and so forth from a large chain.

A career with an independent operation also offers some advantages, however:

— *More chances to be creative*. You will have a chance to set standards and initiate changes instead of just adhering to company programmes and rules.

— *More control.* You are more likely to be in control of your own destiny. In an independent operation, you deal on a regular basis with the people who will be deciding your fate. And, as mentioned earlier, with an independent property you are not likely to b transferred.

— *Better learning environments for entrepreneurs.* Independent operations offer better learning environments for entrepreneurs, because all of the financial and operating decisions are made on-site. If you intend to buy your own lodging operation some day, you will learn more at an independent than at a chain operation where data is forwarded to headquarters for analysis.

Amusement and Recreation Services

The amusement and recreation services sector represents a wide range of products and services from large theme parks to ski areas to water slides to casinos. Many of the types of jobs offered in this sector are seasonal in nature.

Types of employment available in this industry are:

Ski Instructors	Guides
Musicians	Actors, Actresses
Lift Operations	Park Managers
Information Clerks	Casino Workers

Due to the variety of establishments in the amusement and recreational services sector and the part-time nature of much of its employment, many jobs have little opportunity for advancement. However, corporations in this sector provide numerous upper-level management jobs which require a college degree and offer opportunities for advancement. Since promoting events or facilities is involved for many attractions, a variety of marketing and sales jobs also exist. Amusement and recreation services has been one of the fastest growing sectors of the travel industry, including during the recession of the early 1990s when steady growth was still maintained. Executive employment within this sector is projected to increase 39.8 percent by the year 2005.

Large Volume of Executive Jobs

Approximately 684,000 Americans were employed in executive, managerial, and administrative positions in four key travel-related sectors in 1994 and this number is forecast to expand rapidly to nearly 895,000 by 2005. These are top-level executive jobs, general managers, and employees in administrative departments such as marketing, advertising, public relations, and human resources. Administrative support staff is not included in this category.

Given below is a list of Positions available in travel related businesses

Career	Career
Accounting Staff	Exhibits Coordinator
Adventure Tour Operator	Flight Attendant
Airline Reservation & Agent	Food & Beverage Manager
Airline Passenger Service & Airport Agent	Food & Beverage Staff
Airport Meet & Greet	Front Desk Agent/Front Office Staff
Airport Station Manager	Functions Coordinator
Assistant Cruise Purser	Gift Shop Staff
Banquet & Catering Staff	Ground Host/Hostess
Banquet & Sales Manager	Ground Transportation Representative
Casino Staff	Guest Service Attendant
Children's Programme Coordinator	Head Bartender
Concierge	Hotel/Resort Front Office Staff
Conference Planner	Housekeeping Attendant
Convention Services Manager	Incentive Travel Planner

Cruise Director	Incentive Travel Specialist
Cruise Specialist	In-Flight Interpreter
Cruise Staff	International Tour Director/Escort
Destination Development Specialist	Local Tour Guide
Destination Services Representative	Meeting Manager
Destination Representative	Exhibits Coordinator
Driver Guide	Flight Attendant
Entertainment Staff	Food & Beverage Manager

The forecast growth between 1994 and 2005 in executive and managerial jobs in the four key travel sectors is significantly greater than projected total employment for any of the other leading manufacturing segments, mining, and construction. In fact, in the year 2005, executive, managerial, and administrative department employment in these four key travel-related segments will be greater than the total employment in all but three of the manufacturing segments.

10

Modern Trends

Diverse factors are driving the successful 20th century businesses in hospitality and travel to reinvent themselves for the 21st century using eBusiness. But the drivers of change differ in Business to Consumer (B2C) and Business-to-Business (B2B) spaces. In the B2C arena, the desire to strengthen customer relationships, develop new revenue streams, enhance profit margins and create more value are all motivating rapid change. The foundation of success increasingly is the ability to create new business models that leverge Internet technologies to deliver unique value to customers.

The business has moved rapidly and successfully in building high levels of brand awareness out of the starting gate. Loyalty programmes targeting Web-site purchases have now evolved. This new brand awareness and loyalty is a direct threat to the decades of investment in the bricks-and-mortar brands of the industry. As online clearinghouses (businesses selling distressed room inventory) appeal to a growing number of customers, they are directly challenging the hotel brands. The major brand owners have had to fight back. And aligning with competitors in the industry is often perceived to add more value than aligning with the new intermediaries.

Customers' needs do not stay the same. The hotel industry meets the core need of providing a safe and secure home-away-from-home for the business and leisure traveller. But an increasing number of guests—business and leisure, domestic and international - require high-speed Internet access and related capabilities. Guests expect remote-office (and entertainment) environments no less functional than they have at home or in the office.

The new intermediaries have used technology to create other revenue generating tools. There has always been distressed inventory, but networked technologies are allowing the industry to sell it effectively rather than let it perish. There has always been the aspirational non-user of hotel product and services. Now technology is allowing the industry to sell attractively packaged offerings to a market that heretofore has been difficult to identify and reach. Used intelligently, these businesses are adding a further arrow to the marketer's quiver—enabling the industry to add occupancy by targeting specific (and new) market segments. The extreme last-minute decision-maker and the highly price-sensitive traveller are both in this category. Growing numbers of consumers now compare room facilities and rates, and they are learning to bid for rooms and spare seats on aircraft. A third-party can do the aggregation and the constant updating. It can also act as a brand buffer allowing companies to discount unsold seats or unsold rooms indirectly.

The Internet's cost efficiency appeals to companies that currently manage travel offline, and it should lead to an increase in the number of companies that manage travel overall. We have seen the successful hotel businesses of the old economy partnering to compete with the start-up businesses of the new economy. As these ventures get off the ground, they have the potential to cut deeply into the revenue streams of the new Internet businesses, which have relied on commissions and on the sluggish response to market threats of the airlines and hotel companies. It will not be that easy to get companies with an ethos of confidentiality to cooperate with competitors—in the process promoting transparency to common customers. But by pooling their resources, the major hospitality and travel chains can develop portals quickly and at lower risk to compete in this dynamically changing market.

The corporate traveller is a key segment targeted by almost all the major brands. Corporate policy, rather than individual choice, increasingly dictates business travel. Corporate policies will increasingly require travellers to use company-approved online booking engines. These engines deliver two elements to improved margins—directed use of a company's negotiated room rates with their preferred suppliers, as well as reduced service charges for making employee travel reservations. Due to the self-service nature of online business travel booking, companies and travel suppliers must increase efforts to encourage continued use.

The Internet's cost efficiency appeals to companies that currently manage travel offline, and it should lead to an increase in the number of companies that manage travel overall. Larger accounts that are currently unmanaged will increasingly buy online and thus will soon adopt managed travel. Even smaller firms will move their business travel online as well, first encouraging individuals to use any Web interface, then gradually adopting targeted services.

Each managed traveller's company computer will include a desktop icon, which, after entering a user name and password, will link directly to a personalised profile within the travel site. Once business travellers sign on to corporate travel sites, entire trips can be booked with one click on the desktop icon, eliminating the need to re-enter login information. On the road, managed travellers will have the ability to research upcoming trips, check on late flights or change an existing hotel reservation.

Due to a combination of new bookers and the increasing amounts consumers are spending, the online travel market continues to boom. Travel sites, however, face the same challenges that online retailers struggle with - most consumers are not loyal. Web travellers rely upon the convenience, abundant information and low prices found online, and they are willing to research multiple sites for the best deals.

Forrester divides customers into three segments: disloyal, curious, and loyal bookers. "Disloyal" bookers, customers who research and book at multiple sites, search far and wide to find the best deals for their sophisticated travel needs—including the lowest prices, enticing special offers and exacting itinerary requirements. "Curious" bookers research multiple sites, yet return to the same site to book travel and accommodations. The third category identified by Forrester, "loyal" customers research and book at one site. Both curious and loyal consumers rely on one site due to easy site navigation, favourable previous experiences and low prices.

B2B Applications

B2B applications are even bigger accelerators of change than those in the B2C space when it comes to how hospitality and travel companies will do business in the years ahead. Even though many customers aggressively seek choices to meet their needs, some sites attract more loyalty than others. The one-stop-shop nature of online travel agencies effectively attracts bookers that rely on one site for all their booking needs. Hotel chains, on the other hand, may have a harder time attracting loyal bookers because they are offering only one element of the travel package.

Hotel chain web sites can lure disloyal bookers away from agency and consolidator web sites with special room rates and upgrade perks available exclusively online. Although portals have the greatest reach of all travel sites, they get the lowest percentage of bookers from all three segments. To combat online booker disloyalty, hotels, agencies and portals must take lessons from online retailers on how to encourage loyalty. Suppliers must establish dynamic partnerships with suppliers in other travel categories that allow consumers to book flights, hotels, and car rentals at the same site. Hotel chains must sell adjacent categories of products and services. Portals should let the agencies and hotels fight over bookers and instead focus on what portals do best - offer information to consumers.

B2B applications are even bigger accelerators of change than those in the B2C space when it comes to how hospitality and travel companies will do business in the years ahead. The B2B space is populated by many types of companies, including links among supply chain partners and market exchanges selling products and services online to businesses. eProcurement is one example of a growing B2B space in the hotel industry. Adoption of B2B strategies that connect businesses in varied ways is being driven by a number of factors:

IT Infrastructures

Yesterday's information technology (IT) model was based on each hotel and/or hotel group maintaining an in-house IT team, which owned and managed the business's hardware and software. Tomorrow, most businesses will have migrated to an Application Service Provision (ASP) model.

Under the ASP model, providers offer a variety of applications and services to companies, which these clients can access with nothing more than an Internet link to the ASP site. This marks a dramatic change from the traditionally defined "service bureau," which once involved the transmission of operational data to an outside agency for management by a remote application. More recently, the explosion of Internet-based software applications and services by ASP providers has caused old economy and new economy businesses alike to revisit off-premises application processing.

Wireless Application Protocol (WAP)

Mature businesses are not simply assuming that a focus on eBusiness is enough. The wireless market will introduce new competitive elements. Wireless Application Protocol (WAP) is a global specification that gives wireless devices - including mobile phones, personal digital assistants (PDAs) and computer terminals—access to the Internet. The distinguishing feature of wireless service is the ability to identify a user's location.

The network seeks out the mobile phone to complete the call and knows where the holder of the phone actually is. This offers advertisers a dream channel to target customers in a personalised, time-and location-specific way. What are the potential applications or competitive threats? Looking at the customer-facing systems, there is every likelihood that WAP-enabled functionality will be developed to provide access to hotel reservation systems and loyalty traveller databases. In the administrative areas, WAP technology can be applied to interface the mobile sales force with the centrally held customer relationship management (CRM) database—linking the revenue generating and cost generating systems in the bedroom (e.g. telephone, mini-bar, air-conditioning) to the centrally hosted property management system..

Modern Technologies in Hospitality Industry

In today's competitive business environment, hospitality industry executives are faced with abundant challenges, one of the most important being how to lower overhead while revenues are increasing. This has become exceptionally vital for the large 'chain' hotel companies that deal with significant competitions form the independent hotel management companies. In recent times, the hospitality industry has gained from tourists' popularity and substantial overseas investment, enabling the construction of many new international standard hotels and resorts, renovation of existing inns, taverns and restaurants and extended travel operations.

This time for hotel industry to gain momentum of providing 'excellent service' and one of the tools of providing excellent service is through training. There have been a lot of papers arguing some imperative components should be aware of future environment particularly when the hospitality industry moves into the year 2000. Professional bodies have also joined with current research in encouraging the hospitality industry to very much concerned and focused on the customer relationship, how this relationship can be measured in terms of satisfaction and value.

Concept of E-Business

For those operating within the physical world, the concept of electronic business or "e-business" may appear to be of limited significance. But such an assumption could be costly. The financial markets are making massive investments in the companies that deliver Internet technologies, content and related products and services, and the corporate world is now moving toward e-business offerings at a rapid clip. On the business-to-business (b-to-b) front, e-business is projected to grow enormously in the United States over the next several years, with business-to-consumer (b-to-c) trade not as big, but growing just as fast.

E-business is rewriting the economic rules globally for every industry-including hospitality, travel and leisure.

Indeed, it's important to recognise that we are now operating in what has been described as the "new economy," as global trends drive change, including globalisation, consolidation, convergence, technology and communications. Even more, it is clear that the underlying sources of value are also changing. Use of intangible assets such as information, brands, customers, relationships and networks distinguish the most successful companies in the world.

Influence of internet

It is clear that the Internet is having a huge impact on how we conduct our lives and our businesses. And it arrived virtually overnight. In the United States, for example, it took 38 years for television to get into 50 million homes. For the Internet, it took just five years. And for those U.S. consumers that are online, four out of five believe that the Internet is a more important invention than television. Of these same online consumers, close to six in 10 prefer e-mail to paper mail for business correspondence and over one in four check their e-mail while on vacation.

The Internet is also changing the customer relationship-undermining and redirecting customer attention to new sellers of products and services and away from their traditional relationships. And as this occurs, the traditional approaches that hospitality businesses have taken to distribution are all being affected. From reservations taken over the Internet, which are projected to more than double to 9% of volume over the next year, to the declining role of the travel agent. This occurs as so-called "infomediaries" provide information and access, and software robots troll the activity online to develop matches between buyers and sellers, analysing complex patterns and looking for trends for marketers to capitalise upon.

As for the infomediaries, we can expect some of these to move into the transactions business and continue the process of disintermediation. For some hospitality companies, it may be best to join this new competition, particularly if it cannot be beaten at its own game. The reality today is that the balance of power is shifting from sellers to buyers and in so doing it makes the importance of delivering high-quality service, convenience and value for money ever more compelling. The Internet has clearly levelled the playing field by making price information broadly available to the consumer.

Internet business models affect product and services offerings, pricing, distribution and customer service, as well as long-term information capabilities. As a consequence, some hospitality suppliers will inevitably feed different tranches of their inventory through the various channels at their disposal-including the Internet, travel management organisations, destination packagers and the like.

Today's fast-paced world produces ever more stress, and consumers want information and they want it fast. And if hospitality companies and travel providers don't deliver convenience, somebody else inevitably will. They also want to be wired up to the rest of the world-at home, in their office and especially when they travel. And for hoteliers trying to cope with in-room technologies and the delivery of high-speed Internet access, we will soon be seeing more integration of network communication and entertainment products to further complicate or liberate our lives, depending on your point of view. Customers are also looking for consistency-a simple concept, but central to whether a brand has value or not. And in the emerging networked world, aligning the value propositions of alliance partners and ensuring a seamless and consistent experience will only be as good as the weakest link in the chain.

New business rules

Within this new economy, the operating environment for hospitality companies is changing. There are new rules of conduct, new relationships and new criteria for success, along with a new set of metrics. In such an era there are certain traits to business behaviour that will distinguish success from failure. At this stage in the new economy's evolution, these traits would appear to include speed, agility and flexibility.

Speed is necessary to get to market early with a first-mover advantage that assures early adoption by an increasingly fickle, restless and frequently disloyal customer. Such speed is imperative as so-called "start-up" companies come to dominate their chosen niche in extremely short periods of time, frequently preempting the opportunity for those too slow to react. Agility is required to be able to respond to competitive threats by not only those we know and can monitor, but also unseen competitors. These latter competitors may not even exist as yet, but as they emerge, they may quickly disintermediate established customer relationships. And, finally, flexibility is needed to reorganise the established models of business and all of the related processes, and adapt the organisation in organic fashion to a new environment in whatever form it takes.

For business executives at large, one of the most compelling changes that has confronted them in recent years is the potential for e-business. But while the significance of these new media are all too apparent, the business solutions required to capitalise on opportunities they offer are unfortunately not. For most hospitality executives, the essential frame of reference has been a geocentric one where real estate and geography have been the big drivers in a physical world-buildings, dots on maps, markets served, chains.

In tomorrow's world, these concepts will require some fundamental adjustments to provide for market "spaces" rather than "places" as the nature of relationships between hotel businesses, their customers, their suppliers and their alliance partners go through rapid and constant change. As these changes occur, the new economy's business leaders must quickly learn the new rules of the game and adjust their approaches accordingly. And the most successful among us will align key processes around the Internet, build corporate intelligence automatically, create integrated value chains and develop new processes to deal with an ever-changing set of circumstances.

Human capital

Supporting the changes in the new economy will be a vast pool of talented human capital anxious to bring new ideas and new technologies to bear on the traditional ways of doing business and, in doing so, steadily increase the pace of productivity improvement. And if the hospitality industry is to respond to this coming reality, it will need to address some of its most vexing challenges-particularly those relating to the recruitment, training and development of human capital. The human capital inventory for an e-business will require entrepreneurship, as well as visionary leadership, strength in sales and marketing and commitment to customer relationship management. The organisational bias will need to be toward creativity and risk-taking, and away from dependency on analysis and procedures.

In addition to the human capital challenge, many of today's legacy organisations are better structured to work in the old economy, but are considerably less aligned for many activities in the "new." The cultural challenges may in fact be no less daunting than those presented by some of the technological ones. For large organisations attempting a major shift in orientation, the presence of a significant culture may turn out to be quite a hindrance.

In some industries, profits are made on spare parts and maintenance rather than on mainstream products. In the new economy, this business model replicated in the hospitality industry. And for those companies that discount or give away products such as hotel rooms in order to sell linked services, they surely will be redefining the meaning of hospitality. They will also be marketing an array of hospitality and leisure products and services to a customer base that is no longer satisfied with the traditional ways of making such purchases.

Hospitality businesses that traditionally provided room, board, management and marketing may need to rethink their roles in the new economy, particularly as services become more valuable than products. With the rapid growth of "infomediaries" and their facilitation of transactions, hospitality businesses may need to redefine themselves in order to prosper in an increasingly electronic world where one-to-one customisation is the order of the day. But for those contemplating repositioning their companies in an e-business environment, it will be necessary to focus on the current value proposition of the business and determine how it might be reformatted or enhanced to ensure success in the new setting.

In Arthur Andersen's recently published global survey of technology, *Hospitality 2000: The Technology*, we addressed some of the issues that the industry is facing. These included the closed nature of our technology architectures, the way in which we collect information on our customers, our investments in Internet, intranet and extranet technologies, and our adoption of electronic commerce. The results are not especially encouraging and suggest an industry still relatively slow to adapt to e-business.

Only 39% of the industry's Web sites, for example, can handle reservations on a real-time basis, and even fewer still (19%), collect customer information. At the same time, just 22% are using "push" marketing programs and a distinct minority (just 19%), have extranets to suppliers or customers. But these adoption rates are nonetheless projected to grow and we should, therefore, expect our industry's leaders to be far more attuned to the needs of an e-business environment in the years to come.

As information technology (IT) is used to facilitate a company's entry into the world of electronic commerce, our industry's leadership will also need to overcome a natural tendency to be disappointed by the role of IT in achieving competitive advantage. For many years IT was seen as a mechanism to support back office finance and accounting functions. In the future, it inevitably will be one of the principal drivers of value creation in the new economy. But we should not be mislead by IT-in e-business, it will be the strategy, not the technology that will make the difference between success and failure. But having the strategy in place is only the first step. It must be linked to every part of the business.

Planning strategy for E-business

With the costs of playing in the e-business world escalating rapidly, hospitality executives should consider the four phases of what might be called the "E-Business Lifecycle." The first of these-E-Business Strategy Development and Planning-must address the market and competitive context, articulate the vision and opportunity, outline the strategy and the business case, and identify the risks. In recent years, we have frequently seen hospitality businesses put up a Web site on the Internet and consider this an e-business strategy. But without a strategy for this new form of commerce and the business planning process to drive it, such reactionary approaches stand little chance for success.

Once the plan is in place, an e-business design phase can commence to address site design, lay out the business architecture, identify the technical infrastructure, plan for performance, availability and capacity, and deal with tax issues and enterprise security. Following the design phase, E-Business implementation will prepare for the launch with training and change enablement, implementation and integration, testing and roll-out. Once in place, E-Business Operations will need to be supported by IT and audit services, Web site activity analysis and Web site maintenance. Finally, measurement systems will need to be established to monitor performance.

As industry executives embark on this e-business lifecycle, they will need in the first stage to clearly establish the business case for investing in new technologies, systems and organisations by addressing both the cost reduction and revenue enhancement benefits. On the revenue side, there are a number of factors to consider. These include the company's ability to identify and recruit the most valuable customers; the ability to seamlessly cross-sell the company's products and services, as well as those of alliance partners; the ability to retain valuable customers and reduce attrition (especially relevant in a world of questionable brand loyalty); and finally, when and how to eliminate costly and unnecessary discounts through revenue optimisation.

In this kind of environment, the property management system will no longer hold sway as the center of the hospitality universe, but will become just one in a series of customer touch-points that will increasingly include the Internet. These touch-points will ultimately need to be fully integrated into a customer information system supported by sophisticated data warehousing and data mining technologies.

Adding to the industry's costs in this portrait of the future is the cost of grafting e-business technologies onto the industry's legacy systems. At a certain stage, it may make sense to start from scratch and ensure that every system is Web-enabled. This would allow a total interface for a high-growth e-business, thereby maximising the customer relationship management opportunities that it presents.

As to the role of the Internet, its comprehensive reach and ubiquitous nature has already ensured its central place in the new economy. But how should we evaluate whether an Internet application is deserving of our attention? Firstly, productivity on the Internet in the years to come will be vastly improved by much higher bandwidth than is currently in place. And with higher bandwidth will come applications that can benefit from such extra capacity delivering tightly focused and reliable content to an increasingly sophisticated and demanding e-customer. If an Internet application is to succeed in the future, it will therefore need to be designed to capitalise on this coming reality.

Secondly, an Internet application needs to form a community of some sort because without a sense of place, albeit of the virtual sort participants will not have that all-important sense of belonging. And as with the industrial revolution, which drew a disparate population to centers of economic activity, so will such "intranet communities" grow in value as their populations increase in size and their economic product expands.

For larger businesses that form such communities, they are developing new revenue sources and are reinventing their relationships with customers, employees, suppliers and partners. Smaller companies intent on participating in this new environment, may need to be content as a participant in an established community, rather than trying to take on the creation of a community itself. It is better, perhaps, to be one of many players in a successful space than struggling to establish an identity in a world surrounded by also-rans.

Whether large or small, community developers and marketers of the virtual sort will have to recognise that what may have appeared cool in the physical world to generations brought up in the old economy will not work in the world of e-business. Being cool and staying that way in order to get and keep attention will remain a constant challenge, especially for those keen to nurture a younger generation of travellers brought up on MTV and the Web.

Finally, the successful Internet application needs to improve service while reducing transaction costs, particularly as the balance of power in the buy/sell relationship continues its inexorable migration from sellers to buyers. Service improvement strategies will be nothing new for hospitality businesses, but it is noteworthy that service (rather than on-time delivery, price or other concerns) is the top factor that encourages return e-business. This must be an area of focus since the current growth of e-business appears destined to outpace the supporting infrastructure and its related service at least over the short term. But as hospitality executives know, delivering good service can be expensive.

Scaling the types of service response to the circumstances is a growing need, but one that can be modulated if the value of each customer can be distinguished and the response adjusted accordingly. In considering the opportunities in hospitality e-business, industry leaders should take stock of the dynamics that are occurring in the new economy and plan accordingly. It is probably easy to dismiss the e-business world as a playground for others with products and services that are more obviously applicable..

eProcurement

eProcurement is a direct outgrowth of that capability. As a global network using standardised protocols and universal connectivity, the Internet opens the door for businesses to develop international marketplaces for their products and services. Not only does the Internet facilitate the sharing of information, it simplifies the process for the end-user as well, and reduces infrastructure and transaction costs.

The shared nature of the Internet distributes the infrastructure costs across large groups of potential customers, suppliers and others. That means businesses of any size can gain access for a variety of purposes. Distributors or suppliers can build revenue while also realising reduced customer contact costs. Rather than maintaining multiple sales contact systems, suppliers need to have just one connection to the Internet. What is the real potential for hospitality companies?

eProcurement will have a positive impact on business functions and processes for those organisations that fully take advantage of these capabilities. Buyers, for example, have a growing amount of information available to identify the suppliers with whom they want to do business. eProcurement facilitates the aggregation of small purchases, thereby making the order process more efficient and cost effective. And it minimises the need for intermediaries between the supplier and buyer.

Using digitised processes, the procurement process is engineered in concert with an all-electronic design and implementation of the infrastructure required to source, supply, manage and control services. It is one of the most important of business-to-business (B2B) functions. eProcurement solutions were initially launched by companies such as Ariba, Inc., which developed corporate procurement systems for global 2000 companies to give their employees access to vendors electronically. Though effective, these applications centering on "buy-side" solutions were inherently expensive and time-consuming to implement. The new generation of eProcurement is more revolutionary. Today, digital marketplaces create Internet portals to serve multiple buyers and sellers in the exchange of goods and services. These new ventures are levelling the playing field for both buyers and suppliers, giving smaller companies and those around the world ready access, using a Web browser, to opportunities once available primarily to larger companies in North America.

Digital marketplace models

The development of eProcurement offerings, hospitality companies will benefit by understanding the emerging digital marketplace models. There are currently two dominant models:

Industry-specific marketplaces: Organisations with domain expertise in a particular industry—or industry "vertical" in the language of the new economy—launch these exchanges. These market-places support commerce specific to an industry as they seek to aggregate buyers and sellers to reduce transaction costs. Their competitive advantage is based on a unique understanding of industry inefficiencies. Instill bundles eProcurement services to improve control and management of foodservice purchasing, offers a consolidated purchase information service for monitoring contract compliance and capturing rebates, provides market intelligence to manufacturers, and creates an online community and marketplace for small chains and independent operators to improve their operating and financial performance.

Horizontal marketplaces: These exchanges provide a vehicle for many types of buyers and sellers to advertise, share content, bid on products, participate in auctions and manage their supply chains. Such marketplace sites serve a wide range of disparate industries and/or provide them with access to horizontal applications.

Unlike the original eProcurement systems, which generally provided static catalogues and limited sourcing capability, these new digital marketplaces use dynamic pricing models—primarily auctions or exchanges - which are based on demand. Horizontal marketplaces have multiple revenue streams, the most common of which come from advertising on sites. Many of these marketplaces also generate revenues in the form of commissions charged to sellers participating in auctions. Storefront sales to sellers can be an additional source of revenue for such marketplaces.

Vertical marketplaces have similar revenue sources, although they are able to command higher advertising fees due to the detailed information they can collect on concentrated groups of members and subscribers. Additionally, some of them also generate revenues by charging subscription fees to access their focused content and product data. In contrast to vertical marketplaces, horizontal marketplaces face challenges specific to their broad mission. Based on the need to appeal to diverse industries, these marketplaces must satisfy the product, service and content needs of their varied buyers and members, and may be fighting an uphill battle in doing so.

Some companies have been successful using this model, but they have had to invest in expensive domain experts to develop the compelling offerings typically available in a vertical marketplace. The diversity of the industries served by horizontal marketplaces, however, can be useful in reducing risk in the event of limited penetration in a particular vertical. A hybrid marketplace model is beginning to emerge with the advantage of leveraging the strengths of both models. In this model several contiguous verticals are represented in a marketplace. These contiguous verticals can be grouped according to the similar products and services used by all, yet still maintain the content and other offerings unique to each.

Global eBusiness will be fueled by the ability to track the movement of trade goods at any point along the supply chain. Ships transporting goods from Latin America to North America, for example, might be quickly redirected to Europe in the event that bids were greater in other locations. Such flexibility in real-time pricing would greatly minimise reliance on fixed prices. The implications for various segments of the hospitality industry in the following points:

Brands

— Established brands can leverage their relationships, experience, knowledge and purchasing power to reengineer corporate purchasing efforts for improved efficiency.

— These players can develop (or partner with vendors and/or with competitors) private, secure, customised sites for employees to purchase products and services from approved vendors. Real-time inventory management and accounting then becomes possible.

— The major brands can also take control of the procurement process by minimising "maverick" purchases and monitoring adherence to approved vendor lists, ensuring their employees adhere to quality standards.

Management companies and independents

— These companies will gain access to rebates

traditionally only available to larger companies based on aggregated demand.

— The buying power of hotels outside North America, which have had little clout historically, should be increased.

— Management will be able to leverage public access applications that provide access to extensive vendor networks and their products in horizontal or vertical marketplaces.

— Moving processes online should result in labor cost savings.

Market forces are promoting marketplaces that encompass several contiguous verticals, rather than a single vertical focus of products or services. In hybrid market-place exchanges, managers of individual verticals will continue to need a great deal of domain expertise. However, they will also be able to cross-pollinate and leverage the capabilities of other market-places to benefit each one of their industries individually. This will promote eProcurement offerings that are moving toward one-stop shopping, while providing vertical-specific services.

In the medium-term we anticipate that eBusiness ecosystems will emerge as the next wave of eProcurement solutions. These interconnected worlds will allow organisations (employees, suppliers and customers) to transact via a single point for commerce and information, creating a global web of digital markets and corporate exchanges.

Global distribution network

From traditional road-side hotel signs to modem computer networks, consumers have always based much of their travel decisions on information. The travel business -and every other portion of its distribution chain, including suppliers, intermediaries and customers -is experiencing intense competition for the dissemination of information (including price and availability). The entire $200 billion travel and leisure industry worldwide has a stake in how travel information is distributed, and stands to gain or lose much in the emerging distribution model.

As technologies continue to evolve, competing for the consumer purchase will increasingly take place in the virtual arena as players battle for "electronic shelf space." As a result, the competition for electronic shelf space on the Global Distribution Network (GDN) is of critical importance in an industry where perception is reality and service is increasingly defined by technological advancements, rather than human interaction solely. The GDN is transforming the dynamics of the distribution environment-typified by the unrelenting clamor for the best position in the electronic market. As a result, travel and leisure industry companies must reevaluate their strategic positions in the distribution chain.

Direct access to customers, the bread and butter of the existing value chain, remains at the forefront in terms of strategic direction. Indeed, the electronic shelf space can be defined as the "real estate found on the computer screen. Almost all hospitality transactions taking place today, except for small country inns in Europe or the United States, employ some form of computer terminal where hotel availability is checked and reserved. For call center reservation agents, travel agents and individuals booking through the Internet, the physical screen, which displays GDN information, is the location of the virtual shelf space. Controlling electronic shelf space—and the number of "eyes" that view GDN information through one specific portal into this virtual inventory is of utmost importance to the world's leading hospitality and travel companies.

Hospitality and travel players

The hospitality and travel players battling for electronic shelf space can be found in three major categories Suppliers, Intermediaries and Customers. Suppliers contract to provide travel information in various channels for a fee. Channel providers pass the travel information onto the customers and seek to motivate certain customers to use their channel with incentive fees. Individual customers might receive incentive fees from the channel provider and commissions from the supplier. Each player has its own set of challenges for management. Past business strategies do not apply to the GDN. The virtual communities of the GDN have unique business requirements as they are created with players clustering around themes or connected interests. It is these virtual communities that form the "neighborhoods" where customers tend to congregate. Each cluster is focused on information services, products, customer demographics or new business models that take advantage of the new technologies.

Tactics for building the customer relationship include developing virtual communities from strategic alliances between companies such as America Online and Preview Travel. Strategic alliances such as these are creating more attractive virtual communities by providing an appealing product and services. Customer participation is a very important characteristic in virtual communities because it is the one factor that differentiates this model from other markets.

The behaviour of travel agents on the GDS and customers who are currently buying products and services online clearly indicate that companies can increase the volume of transactions in their digital channels. Companies have the opportunity to increase service levels, provide personalised interaction that builds customer loyalty, and provide new services that have been previously unavailable. Companies that understand the GDN will benefit from these valuable resources.

Players in the travel supply arena include airlines, hotels, rental car companies and tour and travel wholesalers involved in the provision of air, lodging, tours, car hire and destination services for travellers. The challenge for suppliers will be to manage and control the multiple entities that make up their GDN. Companies that participate in virtual communities must be willing to relinquish portions of inventory control and capacity management. Existing yield management techniques will need to be adapted to allow companies to effectively participate in the GDN. The rate at which distribution channels are changing is alarming. Suppliers will be challenged to determine the level of integrating the GDN into their organisation. Suppliers in general seem to lack a vision of where the GDN market is going and the role technology is playing in determining the future of the travel industry. In addition, the high cost of distribution is now causing many suppliers to reevaluate current distribution strategies.

Intermediaries

These companies include internet providers, Telephony/ Call Centers (Worldwide toll-free numbers automatic call detection systems, GDS marketing media solutions) and Universal Switch Providers. These switches are communications devices that translate, convert and exchange information between hotel systems (CRS's or PMS's and airline GDS's). Universal switches assist the travel supplier by providing suppliers with "one-stop shopping" for equal access to the assorted GDS providers. The hotel supplier currently is the only beneficiary of switch providers.

Numerous opportunities exist for additional universal switch players for hotel as well as other travel suppliers.

Suppliers that go direct to the customer represent an obvious threat to intermediaries. Any player in the value chain can pirate a customer from an intermediary in the GDN. Channel providers have the potential to leverage strong existing virtual communities by adding new products and services to the value chain immediately. Travel suppliers that create direct links to customers will be able to chip away from intermediaries.

Entities with direct access to customers include travel agents, online travel agents, Internet/online service providers, corporate travel departments, company representatives that coordinate travel for employees, and individual travellers or agents acting on behalf of the consuming traveller. Clearly, the role of travel agents has evolved rapidly as they seek to remain competitive given the growth of the electronic shelf space. In simple terms, travel agents no longer serve as order-takers holding the monopoly on GDS access. In the new distribution model, travel agents become knowledge brokers, serving as travel consultants who add validity and credibility to the information.

Hospitality companies will benefit as they conduct feasibility studies investigating how to build presence on an electronic shelf space and determining which distribution channel to select. In the virtual community, linking multiple suppliers, destinations, and products is effortless when compared to a physical one-stop shopping center. Customers are eager to access all information with as few clicks as possible, whether they are travel agents, corporate travel planners or end consumers. And finding which customers are most profitable becomes an additional task of effective channel management. Virtual communities are much like physical ones, with large differences in interests, incomes and demographics.

Destination Web Strategy in Hospitality

A Destination Web Strategy means leveraging the popularity of your destination to your own advantage by making your hotel or cluster of hotels the "hero" of the destination, and in the same time turning your hotel website into a valuable destination resource for your online customers and increasing its value and relevance for the search engines. This strategy is one of the most effective means to market a local property or a cluster of properties within a particular destination. It allows the hotel to leverage the richness of the destination and shape the local attributes of its environment with creative marketing initiatives that appeal to its online customer base.

The strategy is also an imperative for hoteliers to highlight the property within the context of local resources, because local government sponsored initiatives to promote the richness of the destination, which includes your hotel, are quickly diminishing. Hotel planning is destination sensitive. When searching for accommodations on the Internet, consumers usually use keywords based on the name of the destination +hotel, e.g. "Boston Hotel".

An estimated 85% of Internet users rely on search engines to locate information on the Web (e.g. Yahoo, Google, MSN, AltaVista, etc). Independent hotels, branded hotels, hotel management companies and lodging companies must all rely on search engine referrals. So by having a robust Destination Web Strategy, the search engines will be able to find additional value in your website, catalogue and index the website more effectively, associate it more specifically with various local attractions, lifestyle attributes and aspects of the destination, and drive more business to the property.

Hoteliers able to leverage the popularity of their destination, matched with a well-defined hotel product mix, can capture more online market share and boost conversion rates. The key ingredient is by promoting the many facets of the hotel and cluster of hotels and its relationship to the destination. This approach allows for creative flexibility by making the hotel always the center of attention, the "hero of the destination."

Kinds of destination web initiatives

A Destination Web Strategy can take many forms and shapes based on the particular destination or business environment. Here are the most common types of initiatives:

— *Destination Section or Page*: An optimised destination section or page within the hotel website of a single hotel property or a corporate website that represents a cluster of hotels in a given destination.

— *Destination 1-Pager*: A stand-alone fully optimised one-page website representing a cluster of hotels within a destination.

— *Destination Website (single property):* A stand-alone website encompassing destination attributes matched with attributes of the hotel. (e.g. eco travellers, gamblers, spa enthusiasts)

— *Destination Web Portal*: A stand-alone multi-page fully optimised website representing a cluster of hotels with local area content, pages targeting different audiences (e.g. business travellers, leisure travellers, etc).

Some hotel companies, guided by Internet-savvy consultancies, have already begun employing Destination Web Strategies to counter the disastrous effects of merchant model discounts and better market their product and local destination attributes. Whether the hotelier has one hotel or cluster of hotels, a Destination Web Strategy enables the hotelier to offer a rich, deep, destination focused website with the creative flexibility of appealing to a variety of patrons. These may be: conventions, meetings, groups, business and leisure travellers, lifestyle activity seekers, family, weddings, honeymoons, recreation, etc.

A Destination Web Strategy is an exercise in evaluating the attributes of the destination, the various aspects of the hotel product, and the relevant lifestyle attributes of your existing and potential customers, and packaging it in a presentable manner for the online consumer. The final product becomes a well defined destination-oriented website that serves as the foundation for creative and innovative online marketing and distribution.

You will now be able throw marketing muscle behind various initiatives in response to societal trends, current events, and general shifts in the market place. This strategy is "natural" for the hospitality vertical as the product, by definition, is destination specific.

This strategy involves conceptualising, developing and optimising the hotel website to achieve two main goals:

— Provide valuable and relevant destination information so that the online travellers and the search engine spiders alike find value on the website beyond the mere hotel product content

— Turn the hotel into the "gravitational center of the destination"

— Developing the Destination Web Strategy is a complex task and requires a combination of Internet, hospitality and destination-specific knowledge and extensive research. Some required steps include:

— Identifying the most popular area attractions

— Identifying the relevant lifestyle categories, attitudes

and values of your existing and potential customer base

— Identifying local events that can be exploited to attract guests at the property

— Identifying how local attractions and lifestyle attributes relate to the property

— Identifying patterns of consumer online purchasing habits for the hotel/resort and the particular destination

— Evaluating the most popular target keywords for the destination

— Ranking the keywords according to their popularity and relevance

— Developing credible and relevant copy based on detailed destination research

— Weaving the target keywords throughout the copy

— Developing the "invisible copy": page titles, description tags and meta tags.

— Overhauling your website to add the identified destination, lifestyle and property attributes and position your hotel product as the central point of the destination

— Performing a Destination-Focused Search Engine Strategy

The process for building a destination strategy begins by evaluating typology, attributes, and resources in the local environment. Identify your type of destination. Next identify all the external attributes within your area. The destination may offer outdoor recreation services, an extensive transportation infrastructure, seasonal events and attractions, major business districts, conference centers and much more. After the destination is analysed, begin evaluating and introducing the hotel product and the lifestyle attributes of your customer base into the mix.

The product mix may include: wedding facility, conference room, meetings and reception area, and concierge services, while the customer profile may include business travellers, senior travellers, and even families with pets. The lifestyle attributes are more complex. Identifying the attitudes and values of a person or group, and sometimes of people that you have never seen or heard from (e.g. potential customers) is inevitably more difficult.

Different characteristics of the property or destination can appeal to different customer segments. For example, to the business traveller, choosing a hotel may be influenced by the availability of a function room, high-speed Internet access or proximity to an area corporation, while a leisure traveller may find the same hotel a great location for local area attractions; same hotel, same destination, different purpose.

Index